Praise for this Book

"A must for those who want to jumpstart their learning of SOA. A great starting point in SOA for any IT architect, designer, or developer."

—*Claude Baillargeon, Senior IT Architect, La Capitale*

"What a monumental achievement! This book provides practical insights into next generation SOA for practitioners and newbies. It is a must-have compendium for anyone in the field of SOA."

—*Jean Bernard Mathias, Tolmai*

"SOA makes the world go round! Even more so, with the recent explosive growth of cloud computing and the billions of connected devices and apps. *Next Generation SOA* gives excellent, practical guidance on envisioning, architecting, and designing innovative service-oriented solutions in this new, always-online era."

—*Gijs in 't Veld, CTO and Cofounder, Motion10*

"This is the perfect book for anyone who wants to refresh or get a handle on the foundations of SOA without delving into the deep technical details and implementation specifics. By working from the principles, the book shows how the SOA concepts and goals have matured, influenced, and grown with technologies such as master data, virtualization, and cloud. The book points to other volumes in the series for the depth of detail and technicalities, allowing you to get the broad picture view without any vendor coloration."

—*Phil Wilkins, Enterprise Integration Architect*

"*Next Generation SOA* elucidates the foundational principles of service-orientation in a concise and insightful manner. The core concepts presented within its pages are indispensable for gaining the insight and understanding to become a competent SOA practitioner. This book will be an invaluable guide as I continue my journey along the service-orientation path."

—*Christian Garcia, Vice President, Conning*

"An excellent source for next generation SOA architectural patterns and solution orchestration, reflecting the perceptual mapping and processing of business patterns in alignment with the emerging technological transformation holistically."

—*Ahmed Aamer, Sky Computing Pvt. Ltd.*

"Whether you're a business decision maker or technologist, this book is a great read for those needing to grasp the complexities of SOA and its evolution to today's emerging architecture landscape with real scenarios demonstrating the application of service-orientation."

—*Neil Walker, Enterprise Architect/SOA Specialist, Mindtree*

"A power-packed introduction for newbies and a great reference for SOA practitioners. This book does it all and explains further in a concise manner the relevance of the service-orientation design paradigm for next generation architectures."

—*Abhijit Karode, Head of Architecture (AST), iNautix Technologies India Pvt. Ltd. (a BNY Mellon company)*

"This book is a clear, concise, and very concentrated resource for relevant vendor-neutral service principles and technologies, for API and cloud, and definitely beyond. What I like especially is that this is finally a book that incorporates the heritage of the SOA Manifesto to complement the traditional theoretical approach that many books expose, with real-life mechanisms to bring balance (choosing the right priorities) to the decision-making involved with service architecture and service-orientation."

—*Roger Stoffers, Senior Solution Architect, Hewlett Packard*

"The SOA landscape is changing so fast. With cloud, mobile, and social media so prevalent today, the conversation about SOA needs to go beyond the basic web service. In *Next Generation SOA*, Erl and his team explore the new frontier and introduce the technologies we all need to leverage to stay agile in this fast-paced IT world, which is really what SOA is all about!"

—*Karen Patton, Manager Solution Architecture, Shaw Communications*

"This book gives a clear overview of what makes SOA stand out now and in the future, while at the same time putting focus on those details that matter. This makes it not only a perfect starting point for novice people in our field, but also a great companion to the other books in the *Prentice Hall Service Technology Series from Thomas Erl* for the more experienced SOA professionals.

"Finally, its relatively small size and price make it an ideal give-away present to those who may not be directly involved in SOA projects but still are or should be interested in the subject at hand."

— *Marco Fränkel, Service-Oriented Architect, The Future Group*

"Get an overview of how the SOA landscape has changed recently due to the advent of virtualization, cloud computing, big data, and mobile computing. Without getting into the intricacies of implementation, it provides a quick walk-through of concepts required for executives and IT professionals for their next SOA initiative."

—*Sanjay Singh, Certified SOA Architect, VP Engineering, ATMECS*

"*Next Generation SOA* offers a fresh perspective on core SOA design and technology topics and affirms their relevance for modern industry operating models. It is a must-read for any enterprise looking to maximize existing or future investments in SOA technology."

—*Nicholas Bowman, Independent SOA Architect*

"As I started reading *Next Generation SOA*, I went through a personal confusion in the contradiction I felt between 'Next Generation' and the fact that the book is a 'Concise Introduction to Service Technology & Service-Orientation'. I found that contradictory until it clicked: The next generation SOA is an SOA that has freed itself from its initial dependence on vendor platforms. From then on, it all made sense. As an SOA Certified Professional I have found repeatedly, in the multiple workshops I have led, that there is a loud cry for an SOA workshop for IT top management. Analysts and architects all complain about the same thing: Top management just does not understand SOA and thinks it is just a new coat of paint on an old building.

"Well, this book fills this gap to a high extent: It is short and concise enough to be read by decision makers but gives enough basic concepts on many aspects of SOA to actually understand why things in the IT department—and in the business—just will not be the same.

"The case study at the end of the book—mainly oriented at legacy issues but useful even for eGov—is superb and will give enough material for study and discussions to a generation of SOA analysts, architects, and governance specialists. It even covers SOA governance nicely.

"Just the book you needed for your boss's birthday."

—Yves Chaix, Independent SOA Certified Consultant, Analyst, Architect, and Governance Specialist

"Nowadays, various web-based service technologies have expanded and emerged, offering options to industry practitioners to choose the best-fitting technology for their organization. This book helps you to understand and find out in a comprehensive way the variety of emerged service technologies, along with their importance, key elements, and how service-orientation became the fundamental pillar. This remarkable book, Thomas Erl's *Next Generation SOA: A Concise Introduction to Service Technology & Service-Orientation,* is an accurate and complete reference of knowledge for those who are passionate to explore and exploit the latest emerged service technology."

—Masykur Marhendra Sukmanegara, Advanced Technology Architect

"I recommend this book both for SOA professionals who want to keep abreast of market trends and for professionals who wish to have their first contact with this universe. It is a very enriching and enjoyable reading."

—Claudia Charro, SOA/BPM Professional

"Very good job on publishing/divulging these innovative concepts. As with Thomas Erl's previous SOA books, this one will help people gain a better understanding of the need for service-orientation (not only in IT, but in every aspect of work life)."

—Diego V. Martínez, IT Architect, Zurich Financial Services Argentina

Next Generation SOA

A Concise Introduction to Service Technology & Service-Orientation

Thomas Erl, Clive Gee, PhD,
Jürgen Kress, Berthold Maier,
Hajo Normann, Pethuru Raj, Leo Shuster,
Bernd Trops, Clemens Utschig-Utschig,
Philip Wik, Torsten Winterberg

PRENTICE HALL

PRENTICE HALL

UPPER SADDLE RIVER, NJ • BOSTON • INDIANAPOLIS • SAN FRANCISCO

NEW YORK • TORONTO • MONTREAL • LONDON • MUNICH • PARIS • MADRID

CAPE TOWN • SYDNEY • TOKYO • SINGAPORE • MEXICO CITY

For information about buying this title in bulk quantities, or for special sales opportunities (which may include electronic versions; custom cover designs; and content particular to your business, training goals, marketing focus, or branding interests), please contact our corporate sales department at corpsales@pearsoned.com or (800) 382-3419.

For government sales inquiries, please contact governmentsales@pearsoned.com.

For questions about sales outside the U.S., please contact international@pearsoned.com.

Visit us on the Web: informit.com/ph

Library of Congress Control Number: 2014950931

ISBN-13: 978-0-13-385904-1

ISBN-10: 0-13-385904-5

Text printed in the United States on recycled paper at RR Donnelley in Crawfordsville, Indiana

First printing: November 2014

Editor-in-Chief
Mark Taub

Senior Acquisitions Editor
Trina MacDonald

Development Editors
Maria Lee
Teejay Keepence

Managing Editor
Kristy Hart

Copy Editors
Maria Lee
Teejay Keepence

Assistant Editors
Natalie Gitt
Gila Schröder

Senior Indexer
Cheryl Lenser

Index Editor
Maria Lee

Proofreader
Maria Lee

Publishing Coordinator
Olivia Basegio

Cover Designer
Thomas Erl

Compositor
Jasper Paladino

Photos
Thomas Erl

Graphics
Jasper Paladino
Infinet Creative Group
Spencer Fruhling
Briana Lee
KK Lui
Tami Young

"To my family and friends for their support."
—Thomas Erl

"For my wife, Phitsamai Sisaed."
—Hajo Normann

*"I would like to thank my beloved wife, Sweetlin Reena,
and my sons, Darren Samuel and Darresh Bernie."*
—Pethuru Raj

*"I'd like to dedicate this book to my wife, Tanya, who
has supported me in all my endeavors and never
complained about long nights I spent
in front of my computer."*
—Leo Shuster

"To Petra, my love"
—Clemens Utschig-Utschig

"To Nancy, my wife, and to my sons, Zach and Ben, with love."
—Philip Wik

Contents at a Glance

Contents

APPENDICES

Appendix B: Additional Reading for Planning & Governing Service-Orientation 151

Acknowledgments

- Ahmed Aamer, Sky Computing Pvt. Ltd.

- Claudia Andreia

- Claude Baillargeon, La Capitale + Fondation En Coeur

- José Luiz Berg, +2X Tecnologia em Dobro

- Nicholas Bowman

- Yves Chaix, Independent SOA Architect and Analyst

- Marco Fränkel, Transavia

- Christian Garcia

- Susan Haimat, Dreamface Interactive

- Gijs in 't Veld, Motion10

- Leszek Jaskierny, Hewlett-Packard

- Abhijit Karode, iNautix Technologies India Private Limited, a BNY Mellon company

- Robert Laird

- Masykur Marhendra S., Accenture

- Diego V. Martínez

- Jean Bernard Mathias, Tolmai

- Kumail Morawala, Saudi Business Machines

- Ted Morrison

- Vijay Narayan

- Karen Patton, Shaw Communications

- Friso Schutte, Cerios

- Sanjay Singh, ATMECS

- Jean-Paul Smit, Didago IT Consultancy

- Philippe Van Bergen, P² Consulting

- Neil Walker, Mindtree/Cognizant Technology Solutions

- Phil Wilkins, Specsavers

"I appreciated the peer reviews from other members on the team."

—Philip Wik

"The Mason-Team would like to thank our companies, Oracle, Opitz, Accenture, Talend, T-Systems, Boehringer Ingelheim, which shaped us over the years to become architects, challenged our views, and helped to carve our thoughts—while designing scalable, sustainable solutions. Also to our U.S. authors, who provided invaluable advice and assistance—either through their native language or in challenging us on key points or helping us summarize our thoughts. Lastly we want to express thanks to our families for their patience, for giving us the time for odd meetings at even odder times, for countless customer visits around the globe, and the time to reflect and discover solutions for challenges we—and not always they—find interesting."

—Jürgen Kress, Berthold Maier, Hajo Normann, Bernd Trops,
Clemens Utschig-Utschig, Torsten Winterberg

Special thanks to the SOACP and CCP research and development teams that produced course content from which excerpts have been published in this book with the permission of Arcitura Education Inc.

Chapter 1

Introduction

About This Book

How This Book Is Organized

Additional Information

Innovative service technologies are becoming valuable assets for businesses that need to stay competitive in the face of increasing globalization and market complexity. While computer processing power is becoming faster and cheaper, search engines, instant messaging, and social media channels are generating floods of information that escalate demands for consumable and accessible data.

As the world's economies engage one another through offshoring, outsourcing, and supply chaining, localization is required to accommodate different currencies and languages. Globalization, recession, invention, and communication are some of the driving forces behind a next generation of technologies and practices that revolve around software programs designed in accordance with the paradigm of service-orientation. Such programs, referred to as "services," are expected to do more for less with greater efficiency in order to meet business challenges head-on.

We have reached a stage in the evolution of service-oriented computing where modern service technology innovation is building upon mature service platforms at the same time that proven delivery techniques and design patterns are building upon an established service-orientation paradigm. These developments have made it possible to create service-oriented solutions of unprecedented sophistication.

About This Book

This book provides a concise, plain English guide to the paradigm of service-orientation and the service technologies that can be leveraged to build contemporary service-oriented solutions.

Who This Book Is For

Anyone looking for a simple introductory tour of SOA, service-orientation, and service technologies will benefit from this book. It was conceived of as a brief and gentle foray into these topic areas for those who only seek a high-level of understanding, and also to act as a point of entry for the assortment of detailed technical reference text books that are part of the *Prentice Hall Service Technology Series from Thomas Erl*.

What This Book Does Not Cover

In order to fulfill its purpose as a brief, high-level orientation this book does not cover any topic in technical detail or provide any detailed guidance or best practices on how to apply any referenced technologies and techniques. If you are already familiar with the topics covered in the upcoming chapters, you may not need to read this book.

How This Book Is Organized

The remainder of this book is organized into the following chapters:

Chapter 2: An Overview of SOA & Service-Orientation

This chapter introduces the concept of services before focusing on service-orientation, documenting its history, and associating it with SOA, service-oriented computing, and the relevance of design patterns.

Chapter 3: A Look at How Services are Defined and Composed

This chapter steps readers through a process that demonstrates how service-orientation is applied to shape different types of services as part of service-oriented solutions.

Chapter 4: An Exploration of Service-Orientation with the SOA Manifesto

This chapter explores the service-orientation paradigm through the priorities and guiding principles of the SOA Manifesto. It elaborates on individual statements and associates them with aspects of SOA and service-orientation. Content in this chapter is based on the Annotated SOA Manifesto, which was specifically authored for this book in the days following the release of the SOA Manifesto.

Chapter 5: An Overview of Service Technology

This chapter briefly introduces a diverse range of traditional and modern technologies relevant to services and service-based architectures.

Chapter 6: A Look at Service-Driven Industry Models

This chapter provides a series of brief examples of how next generation SOA practices and technologies can be used collectively and collaboratively.

Chapter 7: A Case Study

This chapter concludes the book with a detailed case study that demonstrates the use of several of the practices, models, and service technologies previously described.

Appendix A: Additional Reading for Applying Service-Orientation

This appendix provides supplemental reading resources for service-orientation principles, SOA characteristics and types, as well as SOA design patterns. This content is comprised of excerpts from the *SOA Principles of Service Design* and *SOA Design Patterns* series titles.

Appendix B: Additional Reading for Planning for & Governing Service-Orientation

This appendix provides supplemental reading resources for service-orientation pillars, organizational maturity levels, and SOA governance controls. This content is comprised of excerpts from the *SOA Governance: Governing Shared Services On-Premise and in the Cloud* series title.

Appendix C: Additional Reading for Cloud Computing

This appendix provides supplemental reading resources for cloud computing benefits, risks, and challenges. This content is comprised of excerpts from the *Cloud Computing: Concepts, Technology & Architecture* series title.

Additional Information

These sections provide supplementary information and resources for the *Prentice Hall Service Technology Series from Thomas Erl*.

Updates, Errata, and Resources (www.servicetechbooks.com)

Information about other series titles and various supporting resources can be found at the official book series Web site: www.servicetechbooks.com. You are encouraged to visit this site regularly or connect to its social media channels to stay updated on content changes and corrections.

Service Technology Specifications (www.servicetechspecs.com)

This site provides a central portal to the original specification documents created and maintained by primary industry standards organizations.

The Service Technology Magazine (www.servicetechmag.com)

The Service Technology Magazine is an online publication provided by Arcitura Education Inc. and Prentice Hall and is officially associated with the *Prentice Hall Service Technology Series from Thomas Erl*. The Service Technology Magazine is dedicated to publishing specialized articles, case studies, and papers by industry experts and professionals.

Service-Orientation (www.serviceorientation.com)

This site presents papers, book excerpts, and content dedicated to describing and defining the service-orientation paradigm, associated principles, and the service-oriented technology architectural model. Online access to the service-orientation principle profiles published in Appendix A is also available through this site.

What Is REST? (www.whatisrest.com)

This reference site provides a concise overview of REST architecture and the official constraints that are referenced throughout this book.

What Is Cloud? (www.whatiscloud.com)

This reference site is dedicated to fundamental cloud computing topics.

SOA and Cloud Computing Design Patterns (www.soapatterns.org, www.cloudpatterns.org)

These two reference sites contain summarized pattern profiles from the *SOA Design Patterns* and *Cloud Computing Design Patterns* series titles.

SOA Certified Professional (SOACP) (www.soaschool.com)

The official site for the SOA Certified Professional (SOACP) curriculum dedicated to specialized areas of service-oriented architecture and service-orientation, including analysis, architecture, governance, security, development, and quality assurance.

Cloud Certified Professional (CCP) (www.cloudschool.com)

The official site for the Cloud Certified Professional (CCP) curriculum dedicated to specialized areas of cloud computing, including technology, architecture, governance, security, capacity, virtualization, and storage.

Big Data Science Certified Professional (BDSCP) (www.bigdatascienceschool.com)

The official site for the Big Data Science Certified Professional (BDSCP) curriculum dedicated to specialized areas of data science, analytics, data analysis, machine learning, and Big Data solution engineering.

Notification Service

To be automatically notified of new book releases in this series, new supplementary content for this title, or key changes to the aforementioned resource sites, use the notification form at www.servicetechbooks.com or send a blank e-mail to notify@arcitura.com.

Chapter 2

An Overview of SOA & Service-Orientation

Services and Service-Orientation

Service-Orientation, Yesterday and Today

Applying Service-Orientation

The Seven Goals of Applying Service-Orientation

Planning For and Governing SOA

This chapter briefly chronicles the evolution of service-oriented architecture and the service-orientation design paradigm it is based upon, and highlights their key aspects.

Services and Service-Orientation

We have all experienced bad service at some point in our lives, whether in the form of soup that came to the table cold, surly flight attendants who made your trip home unpleasant, or customer service representatives who were indifferent to your situation. Thankfully, service experiences can also be pleasant, such as a salesperson that follows through on promises made during an initial sales pitch. People interact with one another to achieve a specific outcome on the basis of an implied contract. As a result, a service with an implied contract is provided with the intention of receiving an expected outcome from the provider of the service, through one or more interactions with the service recipient or consumer.

To effectively deliver a service in a manner that meets the terms of a contract, there needs to be an understanding of the actual environment and factors that will be encountered when the service is carried out. Within an organization, this means that there must be an understanding of the business context. Sometimes, those in a position of authority within an IT department are out of touch with the hands-on challenges and limitations of the business environment for which automated solutions need to be built or evolved. Service-orientation not only enables us to address this disconnect, it demands that we do so through the process by which services are defined.

Figure 2.1

The chorded circle symbol is used to represent a service, primarily from a contract perspective. Each service is assigned its own distinct functional context and is comprised of a set of capabilities related to this scope or context.

Specifically, service-orientation conceptualizes a service as a collection of capabilities associated with a parent purpose or functional context (Figure 2.1). The application of service-orientation to the design and development of a set of capabilities shapes the corresponding solution logic into a software program that becomes a prime IT asset, designed to support a specific set of strategic goals.

Service-Orientation, Yesterday and Today

The roots of service-orientation can be traced back to the early days of modern computing. The 1940s welcomed the invention of the programmable computer, while the 1950s introduced the transistor, the integrated circuit, and Fortran, the first high-level programming language. Fortran's limitations gave rise to the algorithmic language ALGOL, which in turn led to Simula, one of the first object-oriented languages invented.

As an early non-procedural, object-oriented language of the 1970s, Smalltalk expanded on Simula by introducing the concept of messages between objects, where programmatic logic became an act of communication between sender and receiver. Smalltalk further established terms and concepts that were key to object-orientation and, subsequently, service-orientation. These included objects, classes, instances, methods, and messages.

ALGOL also produced another branch of algorithmic languages that included the C language, which transformed into C++ by adopting an object-oriented approach. C++ and Smalltalk sparked a major shift in software development that allowed for extensibility and the merging of data and programs. The object-orientation paradigm subsequently became a crucial driving force behind the emergence of service-orientation (Figure 2.2).

Like object-orientation, service-orientation allows for the repurposing of logic by different consumer programs in both anticipated and unforeseen contexts. The rudimentary outlines of service-oriented computing took shape through the inclusion of practices such as encapsulation, polymorphism, object inheritance, message passing, abstraction, and decoupling.

The 1990s gave rise to Java, an object-oriented, architecture-neutral, portable, and multithreaded language whose development was funded by Sun Microsystems. Java was freely distributed for public use, especially at universities, and soon became a common programming language. Despite the success of Java and competing technologies, such as Microsoft's .NET framework, there were still limitations in the execution of business logic in systems that had been dynamically bound to legacy environments. This led to the development of Web services, which in turn introduced industry standard markup languages that could be used to produce technical interfaces to abstract proprietary and legacy logic.

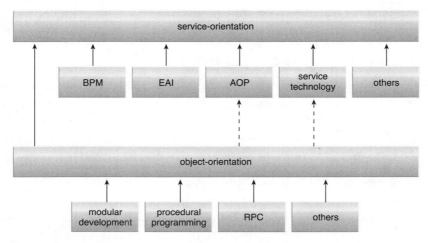

Figure 2.2

Service-orientation is an evolutionary design paradigm that is primarily derived from established design practices and technology platforms.

Endowed with significant flexibility, Web services can accept messages containing content that does not require processing or understanding. Function can be provided independently of the means used to invoke the Web service or the location of the service consumer and service. Distributed objects and the Web had become widely received at the turn of the millennium, as the interactivity of the Web begot secure transactions, groupware, database servers, transaction processing servers, and firewalls.

New methodologies emerged as more programming languages were developed, the foremost of which was a software engineering approach called object-oriented analysis and design (OOAD) that models a system as a group of interacting objects. Each object is characterized by its class, state, and behavior. Notations such as the Unified Modeling Language (UML) were developed to represent these objects.

OOAD was comprised of object-oriented analysis (OOA) and object-oriented design (OOD). OOA applies object-modeling techniques to assess the functional requirements of a system and is performed on a given task to develop a conceptual model that can be used to complete the task. OOD elaborates on how the system acts. During the OOD phase, a developer applies implementation constraints to the conceptual model produced in OOA. These constraints are limitations that are technical or functional in nature, such as those relating to transaction throughput, response time, and runtime platforms, as well as any that are inherent in the programming language.

> **NOTE**
>
> For a side-by-side comparison of service-orientation and object-orientation concepts and principles, see Chapter 14 of the *SOA Principles of Service Design* series title.

Infrastructure evolved alongside the aforementioned developments. The 1980s was the decade of local area networks, the 1990s brought wide area networks, and the 2000s produced workflows and cloud computing. With the transition from components to services, a new era of connectivity and computing power had begun.

Gartner analyst Yefim V. Natis first coined the term SOA in 1996, defining it as "a software architecture that starts with an interface definition and builds the entire application topology as a topology of interfaces, interface implementations, and interface calls." It would take several more years before SOA would receive broad acceptance as a distinct architectural model in the early 2000s, when enterprises began to widely adopt Web service technologies.

It was the concurrent emergence of Web services and the use of the term "SOA" for the branding of a new generation of vendor technologies that associated these two IT trends closely together. For many organizations, the adoption of Web services was labeled as an SOA project. While this association helped put SOA in the spotlight, it also generated a great deal of confusion around what truly constituted a service-oriented architecture.

It took several years for SOA to be formalized by service-orientation, a design paradigm comprised of a set of principles that are associated with the achievement of the goals and benefits of service-oriented computing (as explained separately in the upcoming section). It took several more years before there was significant public awareness of service-orientation. In the meantime, a number of SOA projects failed simply because there was an expectation of achieving significant strategic benefits by the mere adoption of Web service technology.

Only after organizations realized that a completely new approach to the design of software programs needed to be applied was there an understanding of how SOA needs to be built, along with what it takes for an organization to make this type of investment and commitment. This helped to further clarify that Web services represented just one implementation option for building services as part of a service-oriented solution. Regardless of the implementation technology chosen, it is the usage of service-orientation principles that matters, as it is the responsibility of these principles to shape solution logic in support of realizing strategic goals.

Applying Service-Orientation

Let's now take a closer look at what service-orientation actually is. We'll begin with an overview of its principles and proceed to review the primary success factors that need to be achieved for its adoption. This leads us to a brief discussion of service-oriented architecture models and their primary characteristics.

The Eight Principles of Service-Orientation

The service-orientation design paradigm is comprised of eight design principles. Each principle shapes solution logic in a distinct manner to ensure that specific design characteristics are consistently realized. When the principles are collectively applied to a meaningful extent, the automation logic is molded into software programs (services) that can be composed into solutions that can legitimately be referred to as "service-oriented." Every service delivered via the application of service-orientation principles supports the realization of the strategic goals of service-oriented computing (as explained in the upcoming *Goals of Applying Service-Orientation* section).

Here are the eight service-orientation design principles:

- *Standardized Service Contract* – "Services within the same service inventory are in compliance with the same contract design standards."

- *Service Loose Coupling* – "Service contracts impose low consumer coupling requirements and are themselves decoupled from their surrounding environment."

- *Service Abstraction* – "Service contracts only contain essential information and information about services is limited to what is published in service contracts."

- *Service Reusability* – "Services contain and express agnostic logic and can be positioned as reusable enterprise resources."

- *Service Autonomy* – "Services exercise a high level of control over their underlying runtime execution environment."

- *Service Statelessness* – "Services minimize resource consumption by deferring the management of state information when necessary."

- *Service Discoverability* – "Services are supplemented with communicative meta data by which they can be effectively discovered and interpreted."

- *Service Composability* – "Services are effective composition participants, regardless of the size and complexity of the composition."

At the heart of service-oriented solutions composed of such services is the inherent ability to accommodate change, whether it be change originating from the business community (such as new competitors, regulations, or objectives) or the IT community (such as new technology innovation or legacy technology limitations).

Business demands and trends create automation requirements that the IT community strives to fulfill. New method and technology innovations produced by the IT community help inspire organizations to improve their existing business and even experiment in new lines of business. This endless progress cycle of change (Figure 2.3) is a natural part of an organization's evolution. The application of service-orientation principles helps to produce automation systems that can be adapted and augmented in response to both planned and unforeseen cycles of change.

The Four Characteristics of SOA

In order to deliver services that have been designed according to service-orientation principles, we need a distinct technology architecture capable of accommodating the unique behavior and requirements that enable services to realize the goals of service-oriented computing. This is service-oriented architecture.

There are four base characteristics of SOA:

- *Business-Driven* – The technology architecture is aligned with the current business architecture. This context is then constantly maintained so that the technology architecture evolves in tandem with the business over time. Much of what is covered in Chapter 3 demonstrates how the application of service-orientation groups business logic into multi-purpose units that can be repurposed to support changing business processes, thereby staying in alignment with how the business itself may need to change.

- *Vendor-Independent* – The architectural model is not based solely on a propri-etary vendor platform, allowing different vendor technologies to be combined or replaced over time in order to maximize fulfillment of business requirements on an ongoing basis.

- *Enterprise-Centric* – The scope of the architecture represents a meaningful segment of the enterprise, enabling the reuse and composition of services and service-ori-ented solutions to span traditional application silos.

- *Composition-Centric* – The architecture inherently supports the mechanics of repeated service aggregation, allowing it to accommodate constant change via the agile assembly of service compositions.

These are the primary characteristics that qualify a technology architecture as being service-oriented and can further be viewed as criteria for a technology architecture to host services in support of the goals of service-oriented computing.

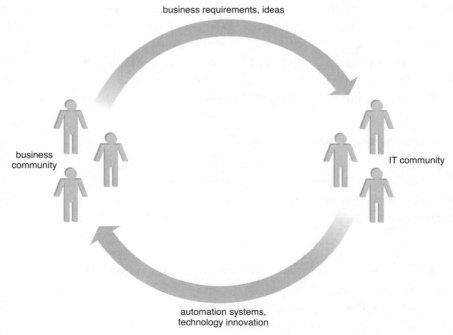

Figure 2.3

The progress cycle that continually transpires between business and IT communities can result in constant change.

The Four Common Types of SOA

It is worth noting that service-oriented technology architecture can exist at different scopes or levels of implementation, with some levels encompassing others. These implementation levels are referred to as SOA types.

Here are four common types of SOA:

- *Service Architecture* – the architecture of a single service

- *Service Composition Architecture* – the architecture of a set of services assembled into a service composition

- *Service Inventory Architecture* – the architecture that supports a collection of related services that are independently standardized and governed

- *Service-Oriented Enterprise Architecture* – the architecture of the enterprise itself, to whatever extent it is service-oriented

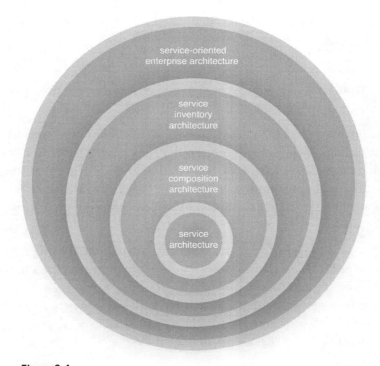

Figure 2.4
The layered SOA model establishes the four common SOA types: service architecture, service composition architecture, service inventory architecture, and service-oriented enterprise architecture.

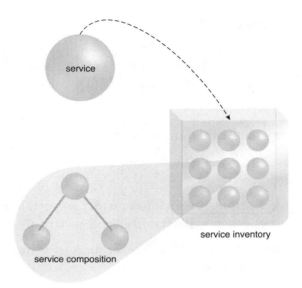

Figure 2.5
A service (top) is delivered into a service inventory (right) from
which service compositions (bottom) are drawn.

As shown in Figure 2.4, subsequent SOA types will typically encompass preceding types with smaller scopes.

Note also the introduction of the terms "service composition" and "service inventory" in the preceding SOA type descriptions. Both of these terms refer to key concepts of service-orientation. A service composition is an aggregate of services that generally comprises a distributed solution or application. A service inventory is a standardized pool of services from which multiple service compositions can be repeatedly assembled (Figure 2.5).

Figure 2.5 illustrates the basic dynamic of service-oriented architecture. Its repeatable execution is enabled by the application of service-orientation principles that shape individual services and standardize them across the service inventory. The fact that services are designed to be repeatedly composed and recomposed into new and different solutions makes service-oriented architecture inherently capable of supporting the cycle of change that can transpire in IT enterprises (Figure 2.6).

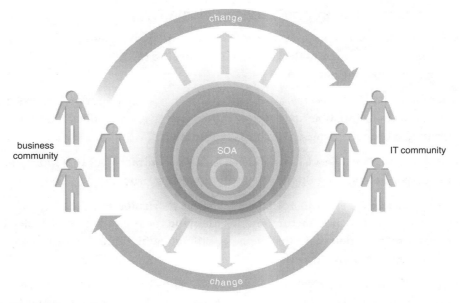

Figure 2.6

When successfully realized, service-orientation and service-oriented architecture fully support and even enable accommodation of the cycle of change as a natural characteristic of a service-oriented enterprise.

SOA Design Patterns

A design pattern is a proven solution to a common design problem. It is a formal means of capturing and standardizing the documentation of successful design techniques and features of common technologies and environments. One of the key innovations that elevated service-orientation and SOA into a new generation of design and enablement was the documentation of an extensive catalog of SOA design patterns , as part of this book series.

NOTE
More information regarding service-orientation principles can be found in Appendix A, which contains a summarized profile for each principle. The principles are individually documented in great detail in the series title *SOA Principles of Service Design*. Appendix A further provides details about the characteristics of SOA, as well as the SOA design patterns referenced in Chapter 3. These three topic areas are documented in the *SOA Design Patterns* series title. Summarized profiles of SOA design patterns are also available at www.soapatterns.org.

The Seven Goals of Applying Service-Orientation

Service-orientation principles, SOA characteristics, and SOA design patterns were created in support of maximizing the potential of achieving the following specific goals of service-oriented computing:

- *Increased Intrinsic Interoperability* – Services within a given boundary are designed to be naturally compatible so that they can be effectively assembled and reconfigured in response to changing business requirements.

- *Increased Federation* – Services establish a uniform contract layer that hides underlying disparity, allowing them to be individually governed.

- *Increased Vendor Diversification Options* – A service-oriented environment is based on a vendor-neutral architectural model, allowing the organization to evolve the architecture in tandem with the business without being limited to proprietary vendor platform characteristics.

- *Increased Business and Technology Domain Alignment* – Some services are designed with a business-centric functional context, allowing them to evolve in alignment with the business, even as the business changes.

- *Increased Return on Investment (ROI)* – Services are delivered and viewed as IT assets that are expected to provide repeated value that surpasses the cost of delivery and ownership.

- *Increased Organizational Agility* – New and changing business requirements can be fulfilled more rapidly by establishing an environment in which solutions can be assembled or augmented with reduced effort by leveraging the reusability and native interoperability of existing services.

- *Reduced IT Burden* – The enterprise as a whole is streamlined as a result of the previously described goals and benefits, allowing IT itself to better support the organization by providing more value with less cost and less overall burden.

As services are shaped by service-orientation, they are added to a service inventory that establishes an environment in support of the goals of service-oriented computing (Figure 2.7).

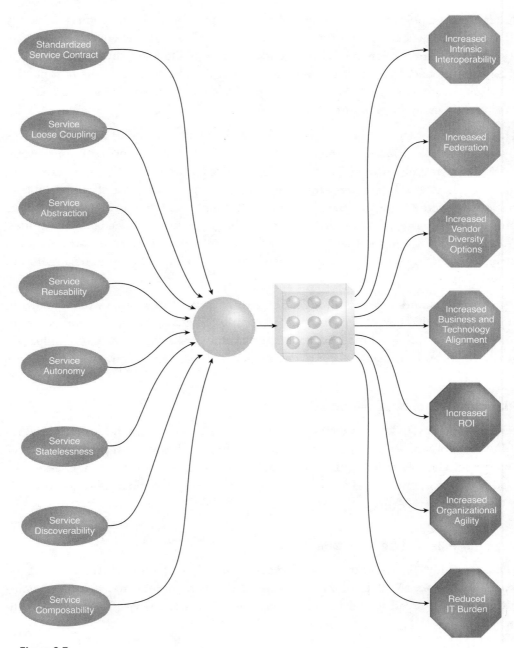

Figure 2.7
Reaching the first four goals on the top right achieves the three strategic benefits on the bottom right.

A key business objective of attaining these goals is to help an organization consistently deliver sustainable business value with increased agility and cost-effectiveness. Agility in this context is not to be confused with lifecycle methodology but rather relates to the flexibility and responsiveness needed to meet the organization's business service requirements and demands. Sustainability pertains to the consistency and durability of execution in line with changing business needs.

The flexibility of an enterprise is a measure of its ability to respond to external forces like changes in legislation, competitive threats, and new business opportunities. Automation of changing business processes provides the ability to rapidly expand usage or modify behavior to improve business flexibility. An agile enterprise should be able to responsively create the automation necessary to implement new or updated business products or projects, as required to adapt to changing business needs and priorities. An agile organization should even be able to efficiently outsource or sell off individual business operating units, and integrate new subsidiaries acquired through mergers and acquisitions.

Figure 2.8 illustrates how the different elements of service-orientation work together to support the realization of service-oriented computing goals, with the vision of equipping an organization with a next generation IT enterprise that is agile, cost-effective, streamlined, and a true enabler of the organization's business objectives.

Planning For and Governing SOA

SOA adoption necessitates a long-term commitment that can demand a substantial re-think of an organization's business and the culture, technology, and priorities of its IT enterprise. The following models and practices assist an organization in assessing its readiness and maturity, and formalizing the manner in which the resources and assets produced by an SOA project are regulated and evolved.

The Four Pillars of Service-Orientation

There are many considerations that merit being taken into account when evaluating the feasibility of an SOA adoption project. A healthy starting point is to assess the organization's baseline readiness using four fundamental critical success factors, referred to as *pillars*.

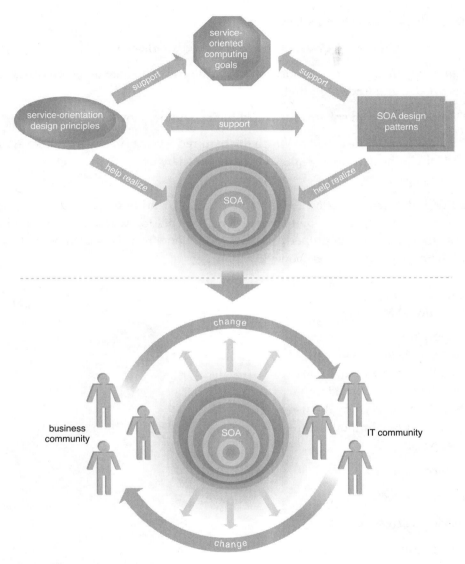

Figure 2.8

The strategic goals of service-oriented computing represent a target state that can be achieved through a method provided by service-orientation. The successful application of service-orientation principles and supporting SOA design patterns helps to shape and define requirements for different types of service-oriented architectures, resulting in an IT automation model that is designed to fully support the two-way cycle of change through which business and IT communities continually transition.

The four pillars of service-orientation are:

- *Teamwork* – Cross-project teams and cooperation are required.

- *Education* – Team members must communicate and cooperate based on common knowledge and understanding.

- *Discipline* – Team members must apply their common knowledge consistently.

- *Balanced Scope* – The extent to which the required levels of Teamwork, Education, and Discipline need to be realized is represented by a meaningful yet manageable scope.

In addition to determining an organization's overall readiness, an understanding of how these pillars represent foundational requirements for successful SOA adoption enables an organization to properly scope its adoption effort. This is embodied by the Balanced Scope pillar itself, as shown in Figure 2.9.

The Seven Levels of Organizational Maturity

Once an organization is underway with SOA and service-orientation projects, its organizational maturity in relation to these adoption efforts can be tracked via the use of the following common evolutionary levels:

- Service Neutral

- Service Ineffectual

- Service Aggressive

- Service Aware

- Service Capable

- Business Aligned

- Business Driven

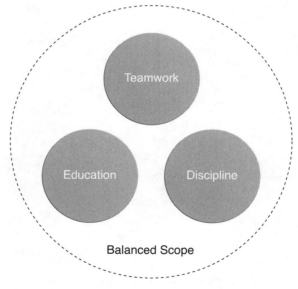

Figure 2.9
The Balanced Scope of SOA adoption is determined by the extent to which Teamwork, Education, and Discipline can be attained.

These levels represent both positive and negative states that may be used to categorize an organization's maturity status. An organization's state of maturity will typically improve progressively, through the repeated execution of SOA projects that are based on foundations that correspond to the four service-orientation pillars, and with the guidance of an established SOA governance system (Figure 2.10).

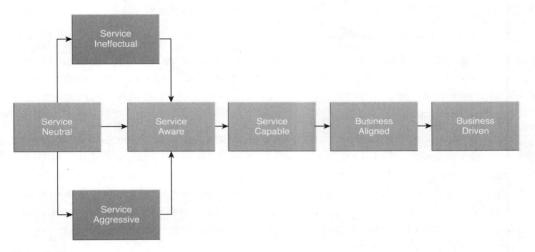

Figure 2.10
The seven evolutionary levels of organizational maturity.

SOA Governance Controls

A critical success factor to achieving the goals of an SOA adoption project is ensuring that a formal and well-defined system is in place to support the regulated evolution of the services, solutions, and other resources and assets that comprise the planned SOA ecosystem. Without establishing such a system, there is a constant and ever-increasing risk that the IT enterprise will lose its alignment with the business domain to become progressively less effective and more burdensome.

An SOA governance system is an IT governance system whose function primarily entails accommodating the unique and long-term requirements of an SOA-enabled IT enterprise. Specifically, a system is established that controls and constrains all decision-making responsibilities related to the adoption and application of service-orientation, via the following types of governance controls:

- *Precepts* – define the rules that govern decision-making
- *Processes* – coordinate precept-related decision-making activities
- *People* – assume roles and make decisions based on precepts
- *Metrics* – measure compliance to precepts

An SOA governance system is defined and administered by an SOA Governance Program Office (SGPO) that is further responsible for the strategic evolution of the SOA-enabled part of an IT enterprise and how its direction and ideas may steer or influence corporate directives.

The journey along the strategic path set for an enterprise is spearheaded by its board, which expresses its priorities through senior management who then mobilize the rest of the enterprise. A high level of coupling between the evolution of services and corporate business cases means that the SGPO can provide guidance to executive management, which can in exchange provide direction to the SGPO. To achieve this level of collaboration, the SGPO needs to be placed in a position capable of influencing the IT enterprise from the highest level possible.

> **NOTE**
>
> More information about the four SOA pillars and the seven levels of organization maturity is provided in Appendix B, which also contains reference information about SOA governance controls.

Chapter 3

A Look at How Services are Defined and Composed

This chapter provides a concise overview of what lies at the very core of the service-orientation paradigm and the service-oriented architectural model: the identification and aggregation of agnostic logic into reusable and composable units. These units represent the foundational moving parts that collectively define and enable service-oriented solutions. Understanding how they are realized and subsequently and repeatedly utilized is the most essential requirement to successfully benefiting from anything that SOA has to offer.

The upcoming sections explore this topic area by focusing on the Service Reusability and Service Composability principles, as they are applied to the early stages of service modeling and design (Figure 3.1).

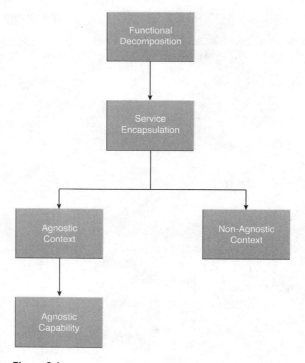

Figure 3.1

A primitive service modeling process that results in the definition of candidate service and capabilities.

Basic Concepts

The purpose of the service modeling process is essentially to organize a potentially large amount of units of logic so that they can eventually be reassembled into service-oriented solutions. Achieving this requires a set of labels that can be used to group and categorize these units according to the nature of their logic. The following terms, all of which are referenced in the upcoming sections, help us accomplish this goal.

Agnostic and Non-Agnostic Logic

The term "agnostic" originated from Greek and means "without knowledge." Therefore, logic that is sufficiently generic so that it is not specific to (has no knowledge of) a particular parent task is classified as *agnostic* logic. Because knowledge that is specific to a single-purpose task is intentionally omitted, agnostic logic is considered multipurpose. Conversely, logic that is specific to (contains knowledge of) a single-purpose task is labeled as *non-agnostic* logic.

Another way of conceptualizing agnostic and non-agnostic logic is to focus on the extent to which the logic can be repurposed. Due to the multi-purpose nature of agnostic logic, it is expected to become reusable across different contexts so that the logic, as a single software program (or service), can be used to help automate multiple business processes. Non-agnostic logic is not subject to these types of expectations. It is deliberately designed as a single-purpose software program (or service) and therefore has different characteristics and requirements.

Service Models and Service Layers

A *service model* is a classification used to indicate that a service belongs to one of several pre-defined types based on the type of the logic it contains, the reuse potential of this logic, and how the service may relate to elements of the actual business logic it will help to automate.

The following three service models can be found in most enterprise environments, making them a common element of many SOA projects:

- *Task Service* – A service with a non-agnostic functional context that generally corresponds to single-purpose, parent business process logic. A task service will usually encapsulate the composition logic required to compose several other services in order to complete its task.

- *Entity Service* – A reusable service with an agnostic functional context associated with one or more related business entities (such as invoice, customer, or claim). For example, a Purchase Order service has a functional context associated with the processing of purchase order-related data and logic.

- *Utility Service* – Although a reusable service with an agnostic functional context as well, this type of service is intentionally not derived from business analysis specifications and models. It encapsulates low-level technology-centric functions, such as notification, logging, and security processing.

A given service inventory will usually contain multiple services that are grouped based on each of these service models. Each of these groupings is referred to as a *service layer*.

Service and Service Capability Candidates

The upcoming process is focused on modeling service logic prior to the actual building of the service logic. At this early stage, we are essentially conceptualizing services and their capabilities, which is why qualifying them with the word "candidate" is helpful. The terms "service candidate" and "service capability candidate" are used to distinguish conceptualized service logic from service logic that has already been implemented. This distinction is important, particularly because candidate service logic that has not yet been conceptualized may be subject to further practical considerations that may result in additional changes during service design and development.

Breaking Down the Business Problem

The typical starting point is termed a "business problem," which can be any business task or process for which an automation solution is required. To apply service-orientation, we first must break down a business process by functionally decomposing it into a set of granular actions. This enables us to identify potential functional contexts and boundaries that may become the basis of services and service capabilities. During this initial decomposition stage, we focus primarily on organizing business process actions into two primary categories: agnostic and non-agnostic.

Functional Decomposition

The separation of concerns theory is based on an established software engineering principle that promotes the decomposition of a larger problem into smaller problems (called concerns) for which corresponding units of solution logic can be built. The rationale is that a larger problem, such as the execution of a business process, can be more easily and effectively solved when separated into smaller parts. Each unit of solution logic that is built exists as a separate body of logic that is responsible for solving one or more of the identified, smaller concerns (Figure 3.2). This design approach forms the basis for distributed computing.

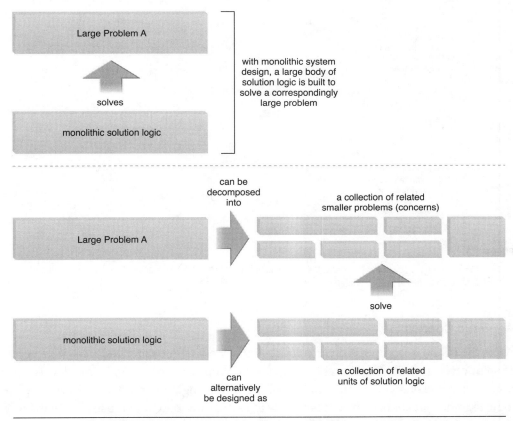

when applying the separation of concerns the larger problem is decomposed into a set of concerns and the corresponding solution logic is decomposed into smaller units

Figure 3.2

A larger problem is decomposed into multiple, smaller problems. Later steps focus on the definition of solution logic units that individually address these smaller problems.

Service Encapsulation

When assessing the individual units of solution logic that are required to solve a larger problem, we may realize that only a subset of the logic is suitable for encapsulation within services. During the service encapsulation step, we identify the parts of the logic required that are suitable for encapsulation by services (Figure 3.3).

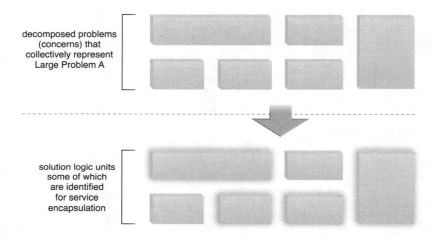

decomposed problems (concerns) that collectively represent Large Problem A

solution logic units some of which are identified for service encapsulation

Figure 3.3

Some of the decomposed solution logic is identified as being not suitable for service encapsulation. The four highlighted blocks represent logic that is deemed suitable for encapsulation by services.

Agnostic Context

After the initial decomposition of solution logic, we will typically end up with a series of solution logic units that correspond to specific concerns. Although some of this logic may be capable of solving other concerns, grouping single-purpose and multi-purpose logic together prevents us from being able to realize any potential reuse. By identifying the parts of this logic that are not specific to known concerns, we are able to separate and reorganize the appropriate logic into a set of agnostic contexts (Figure 3.4).

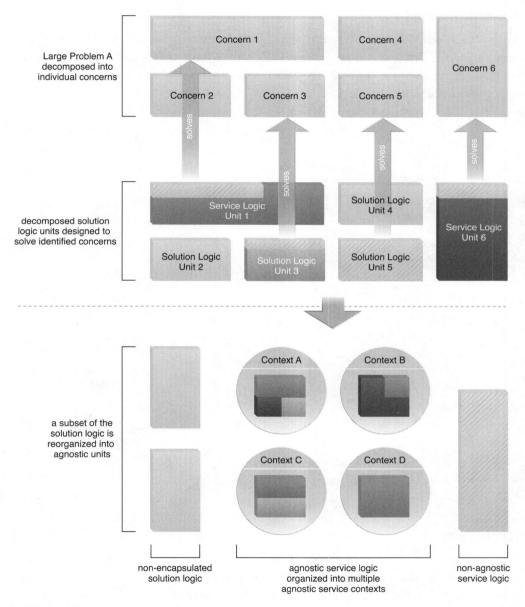

Figure 3.4

Decomposed units of solution logic will naturally be designed to solve concerns specific to a single, larger problem. Solution Logic Units 1, 3, and 6 represent logic that contains multi-purpose functionality trapped within a single-purpose (single concern) context. This step results in a subset of the solution logic being further decomposed and distributed into services with specific agnostic contexts.

Agnostic Capability

Within each agnostic service context, the logic is further organized into a set of agnostic service capabilities. It is, in fact, the service capabilities that address individual concerns. Because they are agnostic, the capabilities are multi-purpose and can be reused to solve multiple concerns (Figure 3.5).

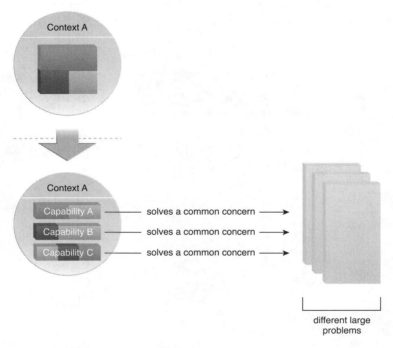

Figure 3.5
A set of agnostic service capabilities is defined, each capable of solving a common concern.

Utility Abstraction

The next step is to separate common, cross-cutting functionality that is neither specific to a business process nor a business entity. This establishes a specialized agnostic functional context limited to logic that corresponds to the utility service model. Repeating this step within a service inventory can result in the creation of multiple utility service candidates and, consequently, a logical utility service layer (Figure 3.6).

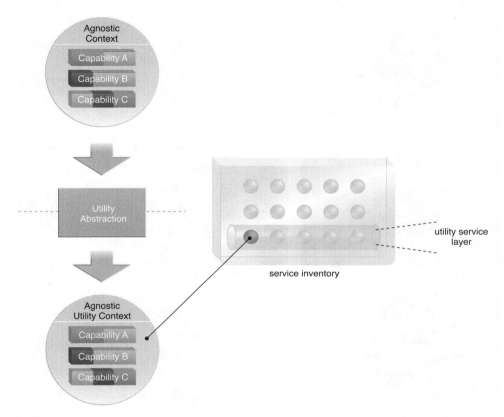

Figure 3.6
Utility-centric agnostic service logic is organized into a utility service layer.

Entity Abstraction

Every organization has business entities that represent key artifacts relevant to how operational activities are carried out. This step is focused on shaping the functional context of a service so that it is limited to logic that pertains to one or more related business entities. As with utility abstraction, repeating this step tends to establish its own logical service layer (Figure 3.7).

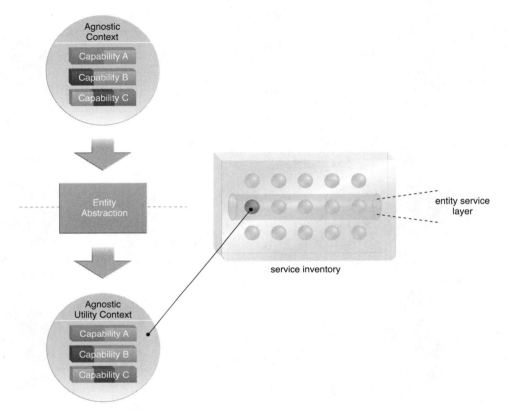

Figure 3.7

Entity-centric agnostic service logic is organized into an entity service layer.

Non-Agnostic Context

The fundamental service identification and definition effort detailed so far has focused on the separation of multi-purpose, or agnostic, service logic. What remains after the multi-purpose logic has been separated is logic that is specific to the business process. Because this logic is considered single-purpose in nature, it is classified as non-agnostic (Figure 3.8).

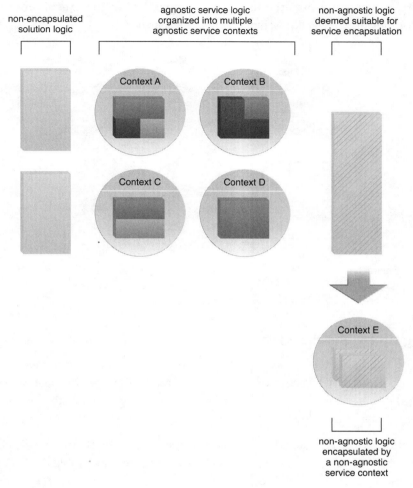

Figure 3.8
By revisiting the decomposition process, the remaining service logic can now be categorized as non-agnostic.

Process Abstraction and Task Services

Abstracting business process-specific logic into its own service layer can result in the creation of one or more task services (Figure 3.9). The scope of each task service is typically limited to an individual business process. The types of logic that are generally encapsulated by a task service are decision logic, composition logic, and other forms of logic that are unique to the business process it is responsible for automating. This responsibility generally puts the task service in control of the execution of an entire service composition, a role known as *composition controller*.

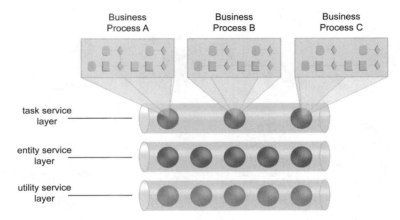

Figure 3.9
Each task service represents a part of a parent service layer and is responsible for encapsulating logic specific to parent business process logic.

Building Up the Service-Oriented Solution

One of the fundamental characteristics that distinguish service-oriented technology architecture from other forms of distributed architecture is composition-centricity, meaning there is a baseline requirement to inherently support both the composition and *recomposition* of the moving parts comprising a given solution.

In this section, we cover several key aspects of composition in relation to service-orientation, before continuing with the process steps in order to reassemble the logic that had been decomposed in the preceding steps.

Service-Orientation and Service Composition

A baseline requirement for achieving the strategic goals of service-oriented computing is that services must be inherently composable. A means of realizing these goals, the service-orientation design paradigm is naturally focused on enabling flexible composition.

This dynamic is illustrated in Figure 3.10, where we can see how the collective application of service-orientation principles shapes software programs into services that are essentially "composition-ready," meaning they are interoperable, compatible, and composable with other services belonging to the same service inventory.

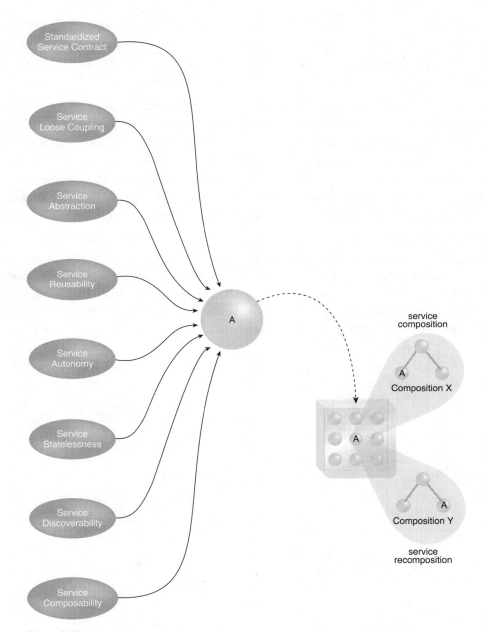

Figure 3.10

Service A (middle) is a software program shaped into a unit of service-oriented logic by the application of service-orientation design principles. Service A is delivered within a service inventory that contains a collection of services to which service-orientation principles were also applied. The result is that Service A can participate initially in Composition X and, more importantly, can later be pulled into Composition Y and additional service compositions as required.

Figure 3.10 does not only illustrate the aggregation that services can participate in. All distributed systems are comprised of aggregated software programs. What is fundamentally distinct about how service-orientation positions services is that they are *repeatedly composable*, allowing for subsequent recomposition.

This is what lies at the core of realizing organizational agility as a primary goal of adopting service-oriented computing. Ensuring that a set of services (within the scope determined by the service inventory) is naturally interoperable and designed for participation in complex service compositions enables us to fulfill new business requirements and automate new business processes, by augmenting existing service compositions or creating new service compositions with reduced effort and expense. This target state is what leads to the Reduced IT Burden goal of service-oriented computing.

Among the eight service-orientation design principles, one is specifically relevant to service composition design. The Service Composability principle is solely dedicated to shaping a service into an effective composition participant. All other principles support Service Composability in achieving this objective (Figure 3.11). In fact, as a regulatory principle, Service Composability is applied primarily by ensuring that the design goals of the other seven principles are realized to a sufficient degree.

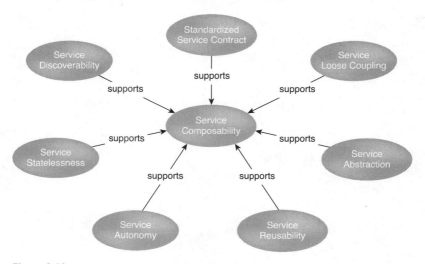

Figure 3.11

A common objective of all service-orientation design principles is the shaping of services in support of increased composability potential.

Capability Composition and Capability Recomposition

Up until now in the process steps, logic has only been separated into individual functional contexts and capabilities. This provides us with a pool of well-defined building blocks from which we can assemble automation solutions. The steps that follow are focused on carrying out this building process via the composition and recomposition of service capability candidates (Figure 3.12).

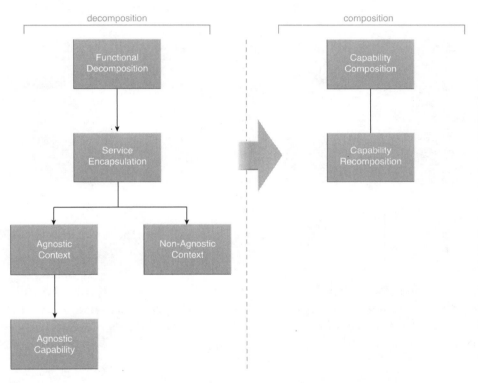

Figure 3.12

Subsequent to the decomposition of a business problem into units of service logic, we focus on how these units can be assembled into service-oriented solutions.

Capability Composition

Candidate service capabilities are sequenced together in order to assemble the decomposed service logic into a specific service composition that is capable of solving a specific larger problem (Figure 3.13). Much of the logic that determines which service capabilities to invoke and in which order they are to be composed will usually reside within the task service.

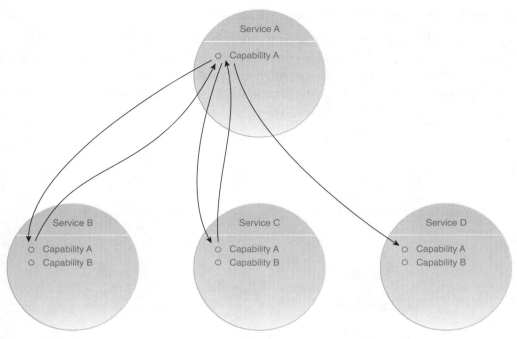

Figure 3.13

Although generally referred to as a service composition, services that compose each other actually do so via their individual service capabilities.

Beyond forming the basis for the basic aggregation of service functionality, this step reinforces functional service boundaries by requiring a service that needs access to logic outside of its context to access this logic via the composition of another service. This requirement avoids redundancy of logic across services.

Capability Recomposition

As previously mentioned, the recomposition of services is a fundamental and distinct goal of service-oriented computing. This step specifically addresses the recurring involvement of a service via the repeated composition of a service capability. The relationship diagram shown in Figure 3.14 highlights how the preceding steps that have been described all essentially lead to opportunities for service capability recomposition.

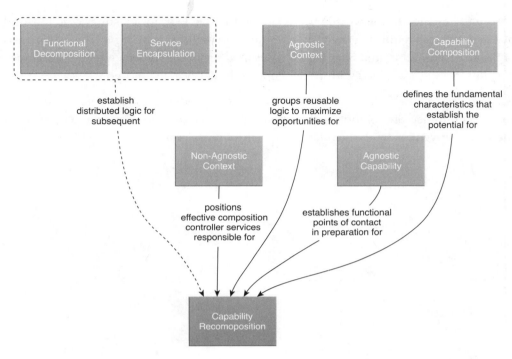

Figure 3.14

The repeated composability of services is core to service-orientation.

NOTE

The seven steps explored in this chapter and shown in Figure 3.14 correspond to seven SOA design patterns of the same names. Familiarity with design patterns is not required to understand the topics covered in this chapter and the use of the term "pattern" was intentionally avoided for simplicity's sake. However, if you are interested in learning more about these patterns, their profile tables are compiled in Appendix A. They are part of a larger catalog of patterns that was published in the *SOA Design Patterns* series title and can be explored at www.soapatterns.org.

One of the key aspects of recomposition is that it is composition carried out repeatedly, as part of a cycle. The decomposition of each individual process executes an iteration of the cycle. This means that subsequent iterations will benefit from having agnostic services and capabilities already available, as the result of prior iterations. The steps eventually change to reflect this by requiring that we look for existing logic to fulfill business process requirements as an alternative to defining new logic. This is the basis of Service Reusability and results in a *normalized* service inventory where redundancy of solution logic is avoided within the scope of the service inventory.

For example, as the first set of agnostic services is produced by projects primarily in support of immediate solution requirements, each service is positioned as a member of the service inventory with the intention of future reuse and composition (Figure 3.15).

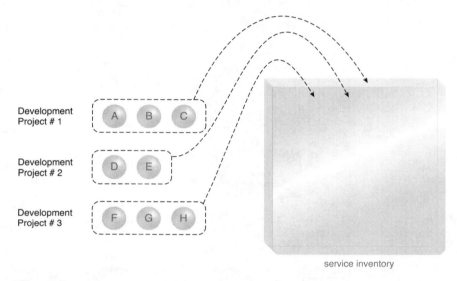

service inventory

Figure 3.15
The service inventory is born, as initial projects begin to deliver agnostic services.

As more business processes are decomposed and more services are added, the service inventory grows. This results in more reusable services that can be chosen to participate in new compositions and solutions (Figure 3.16).

When the majority of planned agnostic services have actually been delivered, the overall service inventory offers a rich choice of composition members (Figure 3.17). Even complex business processes can now be automated by composing services together into sophisticated configurations.

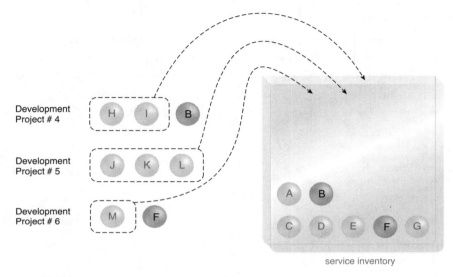

Figure 3.16

The quantity of services increases as do the options for service compositions. But, the service inventory is still incomplete. (The dark shaded circles represent existing agnostic services being reused as part of new compositions.)

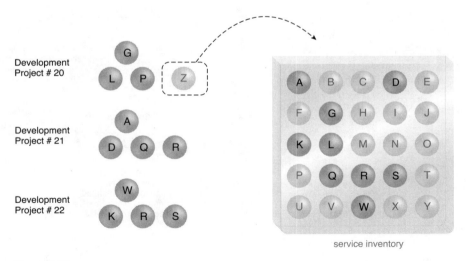

Figure 3.17

The evolution of a service inventory is relatively complete. As the inventory grows, so does the complexity potential of the average service composition.

Domain Service Inventories

It is considered ideal for a given IT enterprise to have a single enterprise service inventory comprised of services that represent as many business domains and lines of business as the extent to which the adoption of SOA was carried out. However, depending on the size, culture, and internal structure of the IT enterprise, there can be significant challenges with achieving this, as highlighted in Figure 3.18.

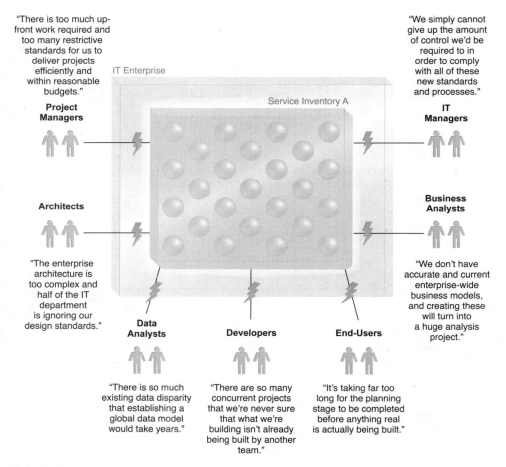

Figure 3.18

Common organizational issues that hinder efforts to establish a single, enterprise-wide service inventory.

Based on assessment of an organization's maturity (as per the seven levels of organizational maturity) and the extent to which it already fulfills foundational requirements of adoption (as per the four pillars of service-orientation), it is often advisable to consider an alternative model based on the creation of *domain service inventories.*

The use of domain service inventories allows multiple service inventories to be created and exist within the same IT enterprise. The scope of each represents a well-defined enterprise domain. Within domains, service inventories are standardized and governed independently (Figure 3.19).

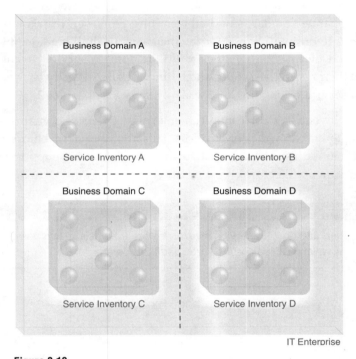

Figure 3.19
An enterprise with multiple service inventories, each representing a pre-defined domain.

Common reasons to consider domain service inventories include:

- The implementation environment is a large enterprise without strong executive sponsorship and wide-spread support for the SOA initiative.

- The enterprise does not have an established, global data representation architecture, and creating one is considered unrealistic.

- The organization is incapable of changing the complexion of its IT departments in support of a more centralized governance model.

Communication between service inventories will likely still require integration effort to overcome disparate standards and conventions. However, this is often considered an acceptable trade-off in exchange for the increased flexibility gained by the domain-based approach. Determining whether to utilize domain service inventories and the determination their respective scopes and boundaries ties directly back to the Balanced Scope pillar of service-orientation that was introduced in Chapter 2.

Ideally, domain inventories correspond to enterprise business domains, such as those based on an organization's lines of business. This allows each inventory to be tuned to and evolve with its corresponding set of business models in full support of establishing the business-driven architecture characteristic.

NOTE
Enterprise and domain service inventories are the basis of two design patterns for which profiles are also provided in Appendix A.

Chapter 4

An Exploration of Service-Orientation with the SOA Manifesto

The SOA Manifesto

The SOA Manifesto Explored

The SOA Manifesto is a formal declaration that explains the underlying design philosophy of SOA and service-orientation. Authored by a working group comprised of industry thought leaders, the SOA Manifesto addresses the core values and priorities of service-orientation. By studying the SOA Manifesto we can gain valuable perspectives and insights into the service-orientation design paradigm.

This chapter first presents the SOA Manifesto and then breaks it down to elaborate on the meanings and implications of its individual statements. In addition to fostering a deeper understanding of service-orientation, this exploration of values and priorities can help determine their compatibility with an organization's own values, priorities, and goals.

The SOA Manifesto

The following is the verbatim SOA Manifesto, as originally published at www.soa-manifesto.org.

Service orientation is a paradigm that frames what you do. Service-oriented architecture (SOA) is a type of architecture that results from applying service orientation.

We have been applying service orientation to help organizations consistently deliver sustainable business value, with increased agility and cost effectiveness, in line with changing business needs.

Through our work we have come to prioritize:

- *Business value over technical strategy*

- *Strategic goals over project-specific benefits*

- *Intrinsic interoperability over custom integration*

- *Shared services over specific-purpose implementations*

- *Flexibility over optimization*

- *Evolutionary refinement over pursuit of initial perfection*

That is, while we value the items on the right, we value the items on the left more.

Guiding Principles

We follow these principles:

- *Respect the social and power structure of the organization.*

- *Recognize that SOA ultimately demands change on many levels.*

- *The scope of SOA adoption can vary. Keep efforts manageable and within meaningful boundaries.*

- *Products and standards alone will neither give you SOA nor apply the service orientation paradigm for you.*

- *SOA can be realized through a variety of technologies and standards.*

- *Establish a uniform set of enterprise standards and policies based on industry, de facto, and community standards.*

- *Pursue uniformity on the outside while allowing diversity on the inside.*

- *Identify services through collaboration with business and technology stakeholders.*

- *Maximize service usage by considering the current and future scope of utilization.*

- *Verify that services satisfy business requirements and goals.*

- *Evolve services and their organization in response to real use.*

- *Separate the different aspects of a system that change at different rates.*

- *Reduce implicit dependencies and publish all external dependencies to increase robustness and reduce the impact of change.*

- *At every level of abstraction, organize each service around a cohesive and manageable unit of functionality.*

The SOA Manifesto Explored

Subsequent to the announcement of the SOA Manifesto, an annotated version was authored specifically for this book. It was published in advance at www.soa-manifesto. com to facilitate discussion of the manifesto's statements within the industry. Provided in this section is the Annotated SOA Manifesto content with some minor revisions.

Preamble

Service orientation is a paradigm that frames what you do. Service-oriented architecture (SOA) is a type of architecture that results from applying service orientation.

From the beginning it was understood that this was to be a manifesto about two distinct yet closely related topics: the service-oriented architectural model and service orientation, the paradigm through which the architecture is defined. The format of this manifesto was modeled after the Agile Manifesto, which limits content to concise statements that express ambitions, values, and guiding principles for realizing those ambitions and values. Such a manifesto is not a specification, a reference model or even a white paper, and without an option to provide actual definitions, we decided to add this preamble in order to clarify how and why these terms are referenced in other parts of the manifesto document.

We have been applying service orientation...

The service orientation paradigm is best viewed as a method or an approach for realizing a specific target state that is further defined by a set of strategic goals and benefits. When we apply service orientation, we shape software programs and technology architecture in support of realizing this target state. This is what qualifies technology architecture as being service-oriented.

...to help organizations consistently deliver sustainable business value, with increased agility and cost effectiveness...

This continuation of the preamble highlights some of the most prominent and commonly expected strategic benefits of service-oriented computing. Understanding these benefits helps shed some light on the aforementioned target state we intend to realize as a result of applying service-orientation.

Agility at a business level is comparable to an organization's responsiveness. The more easily and effectively an organization can respond to business change, the more efficient and successful it will be at adapting to the impacts of the change (and further leveraging whatever benefits the change may bring about).

Service-orientation positions services as IT assets that are expected to provide repeated value over time that far exceeds the initial investment required for their delivery. Cost-effectiveness relates primarily to this expected return on investment. In many ways, an increase in cost-effectiveness goes hand-in-hand with an increase in agility; if there is more opportunity to reuse existing services then there is generally less expense required to build new solutions.

"Sustainable" business value refers to the long-term goals of service-orientation to establish software programs as services that possess the inherent flexibility to be continually composed into new solution configurations and evolved to accommodate ever-changing business requirements.

...in line with changing business needs.

These last six words of the preamble are key to understanding the underlying philosophy of service-oriented computing. The need to accommodate business change on an ongoing basis is foundational to service-orientation and considered a fundamental overarching strategic goal.

Priorities

Through our work we have come to prioritize:

The upcoming statements establish a core set of values, each of which is expressed as a prioritization over something that is also considered of value. The intent of this value system is to address the hard choices that need to be made on a regular basis in order for the strategic goals and benefits of service-oriented computing to be consistently realized.

Business value over technical strategy

As stated previously, the need to accommodate business change is an overarching strategic goal. Therefore, the foundational quality of service-oriented architecture and of any software programs, solutions, and ecosystems that result from the adoption of service-orientation is that they are business-driven. It is not about technology determining the direction of the business; it is about the business vision dictating the utilization of technology.

This priority can have a profound ripple effect within the regions of an IT enterprise. It introduces changes to just about all parts of IT delivery lifecycles, from how we plan for and fund automation solutions to how we build and govern them. All other values and principles in the manifesto, in one way or another, support the realization of this value.

Strategic goals over project-specific benefits

Historically, many IT projects focused solely on building applications designed specifically to automate business process requirements that were current at that time. This fulfilled immediate (tactical) needs, but as more of these single-purpose applications were delivered, it resulted in an IT enterprise filled with islands of logic and data referred to as application "silos." As new business requirements would emerge, either new silos were created or integration channels between silos were established. As yet more business change arose, integration channels had to be augmented, even more silos had to be created, and soon the IT enterprise landscape became convoluted and increasingly burdensome, expensive, and slow to evolve.

In many ways, service-orientation emerged in response to these problems. It is a paradigm that provides an alternative to project-specific, silo-based, and integrated application development by adamantly prioritizing the attainment of long-term, strategic business goals. The target state advocated by service-orientation does not have traditional application silos. And even when legacy resources and application silos exist in environments where service-orientation is adopted, the target state is one where they are harmonized to whatever extent feasible.

Intrinsic interoperability over custom integration

For software programs to share data they need to be interoperable. If software programs are not designed to be compatible, they will likely not be interoperable. To enable interoperability between incompatible software programs requires that they be integrated. Integration is therefore the effort required to achieve interoperability between disparate software programs.

Although often necessary, customized integration can be expensive and time-consuming and can lead to fragile architectures that are burdensome to evolve. One of the goals of service-orientation is to minimize the need for customized integration by shaping software programs (within a given domain) so that they are natively compatible. This is a quality referred to as intrinsic interoperability. The design principles encompassed by the service-orientation paradigm are geared toward establishing intrinsic interoperability on several levels.

Intrinsic interoperability, as a characteristic of software programs that reside within a given domain, is key to realizing strategic benefits, such as increased cost-effectiveness and agility.

Shared services over specific-purpose implementations

When applied to a meaningful extent, service-orientation principles shape a software program into a unit of service-oriented logic that can be legitimately referred to as a service.

Services are equipped with concrete characteristics (such as those that enable intrinsic interoperability) that directly support the previously described target state. One of these characteristics, fostered specifically by the application of the Service Reusability principle, is the encapsulation of multi-purpose logic that can be shared and reused in support of the automation of different business processes.

A shared service establishes itself as an IT asset that can provide repeated business value while decreasing the expense and effort to deliver new automation solutions. While there is value in traditional, single-purpose applications that solve tactical business requirements, the use of shared services provides greater value in realizing the strategic goals of service-oriented computing (which again includes an increase in cost-effectiveness and agility).

Flexibility over optimization

This is perhaps the broadest of the value prioritization statements and is best viewed as a guiding philosophy for how to better prioritize various considerations when delivering and evolving individual services and inventories of services.

Optimization primarily refers to the fulfillment of tactical gains by tuning a given application design or expediting its delivery to meet immediate needs. There is nothing undesirable about this, except that it can lead to the aforementioned silo-based environments when not properly prioritized in relation to fostering flexibility.

For example, the characteristic of flexibility goes beyond the ability for services to effectively (and intrinsically) share data. To be truly responsive to ever-changing business requirements, services must also be flexible in how they can be combined and aggregated into composite solutions. Unlike traditional distributed applications that often were relatively static despite the fact that they were componentized, service compositions need be designed with a level of inherent flexibility that allows for constant augmentation. This means that when an existing business process changes or when a new business process is introduced, we need to be able to add, remove, and extend services within the composition architecture with minimal (integration) effort. This is why Service Composability is one of the key service-orientation design principles.

Evolutionary refinement over pursuit of initial perfection

There is a common point of confusion when it comes to the term "agility" in relation to service-orientation. Some design approaches advocate the rapid delivery of software programs for immediate gains. This can be considered "tactical agility," as the focus is on tactical, short-term benefit. Service-orientation advocates the attainment of agility on an organizational or business level with the intention of empowering the organization, as a whole, to be responsive to change. This form of organizational agility can also be referred to as "strategic agility" because the emphasis is on longevity in that, with every software program we deliver, we want to work toward a target state that fosters agility with long-term strategic value.

For an IT enterprise to enable organizational agility, it must evolve in tandem with the business. We generally cannot predict how a business will need to evolve over time and therefore we cannot initially build the perfect services. At the same time, there is usually a wealth of knowledge already present within an organization's existing business intelligence that can be harvested during the analysis and modeling stages of SOA projects.

This information, together with service-orientation principles and proven methodologies, can help us identify and define a set of services that capture how the business exists and operates today while being sufficiently flexible to adapt to how the business changes over time.

That is, while we value the items on the right, we value the items on the left more.

By studying how these values are prioritized, we gain insight into what distinguishes service-orientation from other design approaches and paradigms. In addition to establishing fundamental criteria that we can use to determine how compatible service-orientation is for a given organization, it can further help determine the extent to which service-orientation can or should be adopted.

An appreciation of the core values can also help us understand how challenging it may be to successfully carry out SOA projects within certain environments. For example, several of these prioritizations may clash head-on with established beliefs and preferences. In such a case, the benefits of service-orientation need to be weighed against the effort and impact their adoption may have (not just on technology, but also on the organization and IT culture).

The upcoming guiding principles were provided to help address many of these types of challenges.

Guiding Principles

We follow these principles:

So far, the manifesto has established an overall vision as well as a set of core values associated with the vision. The remainder of the declaration is comprised of a set of principles that are provided as guidance for adhering to the values and realizing the vision.

It's important to keep in mind that these are *guiding* principles that were authored specifically in support of this manifesto. They are not to be confused with the *design* principles that comprise service-orientation.

Respect the social and power structure of the organization.

One of the most common SOA pitfalls is approaching adoption as a technology-centric initiative. Doing so almost always leads to failure because we are simply not prepared for the inevitable organizational impacts.

The adoption of service-orientation is about transforming the way we automate business. However, regardless of what plans we may have for making this transformation effort happen, we must always begin with an understanding and an appreciation of the organization, its structure, its goals, and its culture.

The adoption of service-orientation is very much a human experience. It requires support from those in authority and asks that the IT culture adopt a strategic, community-centric mindset. We must fully acknowledge and plan for this level of organizational change in order to receive the necessary long-term commitments required to achieve the target state of service-orientation.

These types of considerations not only help us determine how to best proceed with an SOA initiative, they further assist us in defining the most appropriate scope and approach for adoption.

Recognize that SOA ultimately demands change on many levels.

There's a saying that goes: "Success is being prepared for opportunity." Perhaps the number one lesson learned from SOA projects that have been carried out in the past is that we must fully comprehend and then plan and prepare for the volume and range of change that is brought about as a result of adopting service-orientation. Here are some examples.

Service-orientation changes how we build automation solutions by positioning software programs as IT assets with long-term, repeatable business value. Depending on the extent to which cloud-based infrastructure may be leveraged, a significant up-front investment may be required to create an environment comprised of such assets. Furthermore, an ongoing commitment is required to maintain and leverage their value. So, right out of the gate, changes are required to how we fund, measure, and maintain systems within the IT enterprise.

Additionally, because service-orientation introduces services that are positioned as resources of the enterprise, there will be changes in how we own different parts of systems and regulate their design and usage, not to mention changes to the infrastructure required to guarantee continuous scalability and reliability. Mature SOA governance systems and the service technologies covered in the subsequent chapters address these concerns.

The scope of SOA adoption can vary. Keep efforts manageable and within meaningful boundaries.

A common myth has been that in order to realize the strategic goals of service-oriented computing, service-orientation must be adopted on an enterprise-wide basis. This means establishing and enforcing design and industry standards across the IT enterprise so as to create an enterprise-wide inventory of intrinsically interoperable services. While there is nothing wrong with this ideal, it is not a realistic goal for many organizations, especially those with larger IT enterprises.

The most appropriate scope for any given SOA adoption effort needs to be determined as a result of planning and analysis in conjunction with pragmatic considerations, such as the aforementioned impacts on organizational structures, areas of authority, and cultural changes that are brought about. Taking the Balanced Scope pillar into account during the planning stages assists in determining a suitable, initial adoption scope based on an organization's maturity and readiness.

These factors further help determine a scope of adoption that is deemed manageable. But for any adoption effort to result in an environment that progresses the IT enterprise toward the desired strategic target state, the scope must also be meaningful. In other words, it must be meaningfully cross-silo so that collections of services can be delivered in relation to each other within a pre-defined boundary. In other words, we want to create "continents of services," not the dreaded "islands of services."

This concept of building independently owned and governed service inventories within domains of the same IT enterprise is based on the Domain Inventory design pattern that was originally published as part of the SOA design patterns catalog at www.soapatterns.org. This approach reduces many of the risks that are commonly attributed to "big-bang" SOA projects and furthermore mitigates the impact of both organizational and technological changes (because the impact is limited to a segmented and managed scope). It is also an approach that allows for phased adoption where one domain service inventory can be established at a time.

Products and standards alone will neither give you SOA nor apply the service-orientation paradigm for you.

This guiding principle addresses two separate but very much related myths. The first is that you can buy your way into SOA with modern technology products, and the second is the assumption that the adoption of industry standards (such as XML, WSDL, SCA, etc.) will naturally result in service-oriented technology architecture.

The vendor and industry standards communities have been credited with building modern service technology innovation upon non-proprietary frameworks and platforms. Everything from service virtualization to cloud computing and grid computing has helped advance the potential for building sophisticated and complex service-oriented solutions. However, none of these technologies are exclusive to SOA. You can just as easily build silo-based systems in the cloud as you can on your own private servers.

There is no such thing as "SOA in a box" because in order to achieve service-oriented technology architecture, service-orientation needs to be successfully applied; this, in turn, requires everything that we design and build to be driven by the unique direction, vision, and requirements of the business.

SOA can be realized through a variety of technologies and standards.

Service-orientation is a technology-neutral and vendor-neutral paradigm. Service-oriented architecture is a technology-neutral and vendor-neutral architectural model. Service-oriented computing can be viewed as a specialized form of distributed computing. Service-oriented solutions can therefore be built using just about any technology and industry standard suitable for distributed computing.

While some technologies (especially those based on industry standards) can increase the potential of applying some service-orientation design principles, it is really the potential to fulfill business requirements that ultimately determines the most suitable choice of technologies and industry standards. SOA design patterns, such as Dual

Protocols and Concurrent Contracts, support the use and standardization of alternative service technologies within the same service inventory.

Establish a uniform set of enterprise standards and policies based on industry, de facto, and community standards.

Industry standards represent non-proprietary technology specifications that help establish, among other things, consistent baseline characteristics (such as transport, interface, message format, etc.) of technology architecture. However, the use of industry standards alone does not guarantee that services will be intrinsically interoperable.

For two software programs to be fully compatible, additional conventions (such as data models and policies) need to be adhered to. This is why IT enterprises must establish and enforce design standards. Failure to properly standardize and regulate the standardization of services within a given domain will begin to tear at the fabric of interoperability upon which the realization of many strategic benefits relies.

This guiding principle advocates the use of enterprise design standards and design principles, such as Standardized Service Contract and Service Loose Coupling. It also reminds us that, whenever possible and feasible, custom design standards should be based upon and incorporate standards and service-orientation design principles already in use by the industry and the community in general.

Pursue uniformity on the outside while allowing diversity on the inside.

Federation can be defined as the unification of a set of disparate entities. While allowing each entity to be independently governed on the inside, all agree to adhere to a common, unified front.

A fundamental part of service-oriented architecture is the introduction of a federated endpoint layer that abstracts service implementation details while publishing a set of endpoints that represent individual services within a given domain in a unified manner. Accomplishing this generally involves achieving unity based on a combination of industry and design standards. The consistency of this unity across services is key to realizing intrinsic interoperability, as it represents the primary purpose and responsibility of the Standardized Service Contract design principle.

A federated endpoint layer further helps increase opportunities to explore vendor-diversity options. For example, one service may need to be built upon a completely different platform than another. As long as these services maintain compatible end-points, the governance of their respective implementations can remain independent. This not only highlights that services can be built using different implementation mediums (such as EJB, .NET, SOAP, REST, etc.), it also emphasizes that different intermediary platforms and technologies can be utilized together, as required.

Note that this type of diversity comes with a price. This principle does not advocate diversification itself—it simply recommends that we allow diversification when justified, so that "best-of-breed" technologies and platforms can be leveraged to maximize fulfillment of business requirements.

Identify services through collaboration with business and technology stakeholders.

In order for technology solutions to be business-driven, the technology must be in sync with the business. Therefore, another goal of service-oriented computing is to align technology and business via the application of service-orientation. The stage at which this alignment is initially accomplished is during the analysis and modeling processes that usually precede actual service development and delivery.

The critical ingredient to carrying out service-oriented analysis is to have both business and technology experts working hand-in-hand to identify and define candidate services. For example, business experts can help accurately define functional contexts pertaining to business-centric services, while technology experts can provide pragmatic input to ensure that the granularity and definition of conceptual services remains realistic in relation to their eventual implementation environments.

Maximize service usage by considering the current and future scope of utilization.

The extent of a given SOA project may be enterprise-wide or may be limited to a domain of the enterprise. Whatever the scope, a pre-defined boundary is established to encompass an inventory of services that need to be conceptually modeled before they can be developed. By modeling multiple services in relation to each other, we essentially establish a blueprint of the services we will eventually be building. This exercise is critical when attempting to identify and define services that can be shared by different solutions.

There are various methodologies and approaches that can be used to carry out service-oriented analysis stages. However, a common thread among all of them is that the functional boundaries of services be normalized to avoid redundancy. Even then, normalized services do not necessarily make for highly reusable services. Other factors come into play, such as service granularity, autonomy, state management, scalability, composability, and the extent to which service logic is sufficiently generic so that it can be effectively reused.

These types of considerations as guided by business and technology expertise provide the opportunity to define services that capture current utilization requirements while possessing the flexibility to adapt to future change.

Verify that services satisfy business requirements and goals.

As with anything, services can be misused. When growing and managing a portfolio of services, their usage and effectiveness at fulfilling business requirements need to be verified and measured. Modern tools provide various means of monitoring service usage, but there are intangibles that also need to be taken into consideration to ensure that services are not just used because they are available but are truly fulfilling business needs and meeting expectations.

This is especially true with shared services that shoulder multiple dependencies. Not only do shared services require adequate infrastructure to guarantee scalability and reliability for all of the solutions that reuse them, they also need to be designed and extended with great care to ensure their functional contexts are never skewed.

Evolve services and their organization in response to real use.

This guiding principle ties directly back to the "Evolutionary refinement over pursuit of initial perfection" value statement, as well as the overall goal of maintaining an alignment of business and technology.

We can never expect to rely on guesswork when it comes to determining service granularity, the range of functions that services need to perform, or how services will need to be organized into compositions. Based on whatever extent of analysis we are able to initially perform, a given service will be assigned a defined functional context and will contain one or more functional capabilities that likely involve it in one or more service compositions.

As real-world business requirements and circumstances change, the service may need to be augmented, extended, refactored, or perhaps even replaced. Service-orientation design principles build native flexibility into service architectures so that, as software programs, services are resilient and adaptive to change and to being changed in response to real-world usage.

Separate the different aspects of a system that change at different rates.

What makes monolithic and silo-based systems inflexible is that change can have a significant impact on their existing usage. This is why it is often easier to create new silo-based applications rather than augment or extend existing ones.

The rationale behind the separation of concerns theory is that a larger problem can be more effectively solved when decomposed into a set of smaller problems or concerns. When applying service-orientation to the separation of concerns, we build corresponding units of solution logic that solve individual concerns, thereby allowing us to aggregate the units to solve the larger problem in addition to giving us the opportunity to aggregate them into different configurations in order to solve other problems.

Besides fostering service reusability, this approach introduces numerous layers of abstraction that help shield service-comprised systems from the impacts of change. This form of abstraction can exist at different levels. For example, if legacy resources encapsulated by one service need to be replaced, the impact of that change can be mitigated as long as the service is able to retain its original endpoint and functional behavior.

Another example is the separation of agnostic from non-agnostic logic. The former type of logic has high reuse potential if it is multi-purpose and less likely to change. Non-agnostic logic, on the other hand, typically represents the single-purpose parts of parent business process logic, which are often more volatile. Separating these respective logic types into different service layers further introduces abstraction that enables service reusability while shielding services, and any solutions that utilize them, from the impacts of change.

Reduce implicit dependencies and publish all external dependencies to increase robustness and reduce the impact of change.

This guiding principle embodies the purpose of the Service Loose Coupling design principle. How a service architecture is internally structured and how services relate to programs that consume them (which can include other services) all comes down to dependencies that are formed on individually moving parts that are part of the service architecture.

Layers of abstraction help ease evolutionary change by localizing the impacts of the change to controlled regions. For example, within service architectures, service façades can be used to abstract parts of the implementation in order to minimize the reach of implementation dependencies.

On the other hand, published technical service contracts need to disclose the dependencies that service consumers must form in order to interact with services. As per the Service Abstraction principle, the reduction of internal dependencies that can affect these technical contracts when change does occur minimizes the proliferation of the impact of those changes upon dependent service consumers.

At every level of abstraction, organize each service around a cohesive and manageable unit of functionality.

Each service requires a well-defined functional context that determines what logic does and does not belong within the service's functional boundary. Determining the scope and granularity of these functional service boundaries is one of the most critical responsibilities during the service delivery lifecycle.

Services with coarse functional granularity may be too inflexible to be effective, especially if they are expected to be reusable. On the other hand, overly fine-grained services may tax an infrastructure in that service compositions will need to consist of increased quantities of composition members.

Determining the right balance of functional scope and granularity requires a combination of business and technology expertise, and further requires an understanding of how services within a given boundary relate to each other.

Many of the guiding principles described in this manifesto help to make this determination in support of positioning each service as an IT asset that is capable of furthering an IT enterprise toward that target state whereby the strategic benefits of service-oriented computing are realized.

Ultimately, though, it is the attainment of real-world business value that dictates, from conception to delivery to repeated usage, the evolutionary path of any unit of service-oriented functionality.

Chapter 5

An Overview of Service Technology

SOA implementations can consist of a combination of technologies, products, APIs, and supporting infrastructure extensions. The composition of a deployed SOA is unique within each enterprise, and an SOA implementation can be further typified by introducing new technologies and platforms that support creating, executing, and evolving service-oriented solutions. As a result, building a technical architecture in support of the service-oriented architectural model establishes an environment suitable for solution logic that has been designed in compliance with service-orientation design principles.

Service-oriented solutions can be highly reliant on the sharing of common infrastructure across shared services and service-oriented solutions. The best way to understand the distinct characteristics of service infrastructure is to compare it to the traditional silo approach to application development, where the up-front costs required for applications to manage most environment functions are low, and costs for additional new applications are high.

A next generation service technology environment typically uses common software infrastructure components to perform housekeeping and general business functions for solutions, and the shared infrastructure layer provides further features and extensions. The initial costs of building such IT infrastructure can be significant, unless leased cloud-based IT resources are used. Either way, the costs of adding additional business functionality are lower than for a silo approach and continue to decrease as service technologies mature into commercial commodities.

Web-Based Services

A Web-based service is a self-contained body of solution logic that provides a physically decoupled technical contract that can be published and accessed using Web-based technologies. Web-based services support interoperable machine-to-machine interaction over a network, and are often designed to communicate with non-proprietary technologies based on industry standards.

There are two common Web-based service technologies:

SOAP-Based Web Services

A SOAP-based Web service (also known as simply a "Web service") relies on communication via the SOAP industry standard and typically contains a published technical contract defined using the Web Services Description Language (WSDL) and XML Schema Definition Language (XML Schema) industry standards.

There are many additional industry standards that provide sophisticated extensions to the contract definition and runtime functionality of SOAP-based Web services. These extensions are collectively referred to as WS-* extensions or standards and encompass interoperability standards, such as those provided by the WS-I. Examples of the types of features available via WS-* industry standards include security, transactions, and policies.

REST Services

Representational State Transfer (REST) is an architectural style based on the underlying architecture of the World Wide Web. Unlike SOAP-based Web services architecture, which is primarily based on the combined usage of the aforementioned industry standards, REST is based on an architectural style defined by goals and constraints.

REST services do not have individual service contracts but instead share a uniform contract, most commonly via the standard HTTP protocol. REST services typically communicate with each other using HTTP methods provided by the uniform contract. REST services within the same service inventory generally share the same uniform contract. When REST services exchange data, HTTP headers are used to carry metadata, such as security codes, authentication tokens, response codes, and error information. Data exchanged by REST services can also be defined using XML schemas.

REST services may work in combination with other technologies, such as JavaScript Object Notation (JSON) and the Open Data Protocol (OData). A lightweight and compressed alternative to XML for bundling data, JSON is translated into XML through a server-side component that resides near the front end to communicate with XML-based services and transport data from back-end systems into front-end forms. OData is a protocol for the retrieval and transport of data structures.

Components

As an alternative to Web-based implementation mediums, services can be built using traditional component-based technology. A component is essentially a software program designed to be part of a distributed system that provides a technical interface comparable to a traditional API, through which it exposes public capabilities as methods that allow it to be explicitly invoked by other programs. Components generally rely on proprietary, platform-specific development and runtime technologies and communicate using binary protocols. For example, a component can be built using Java or .NET tools to be deployed in a runtime environment that is capable of supporting the communications technology requirements of the component, as implemented by the chosen development platform.

Service Virtualization

Virtualization is an established technology that has enabled hardware owners to repeatedly leverage physical servers for wide, concurrent usage. Service virtualization separates the core service logic from the details of its invocation as a service. Virtualization allows physical IT resources to provide multiple virtual images of themselves so that their underlying processing capabilities can be shared individually by multiple consumers.

Services are typically hosted by a virtual server, which is a form of virtualization software that emulates a physical server including its operating system. Each physical server can host multiple virtual servers using a core virtualization platform known as the hypervisor. Sophisticated failover technology exists that allows service implementations to be moved between servers and for redundant service implementations to be distributed across servers.

Service-based solutions can involve service implementations based on a variety of technologies, such as .NET and Java. These implementations need to be configured, managed, and enabled for communication. As such, new services can be programmed to run as components in a service container, in order to provide relevant features so that they can be invoked and in turn invoke other services. The degree of separation of the service logic from its communication with other services determines the effectiveness of service virtualization.

Cloud Computing

Cloud computing is defined as a specialized form of distributed computing that introduces utilization models for remotely provisioning scalable and measured IT resources. Clouds rely heavily on virtualization technology to remotely provision commodity IT resources that are commonly made available for lease via pay-per-usage models.

Cloud computing is a vast field that encompasses many technologies, models, and architectures. Organizations can move entire data centers and enterprise infrastructures into cloud environments from where they can benefit from access to massive amounts of IT resources. Alternatively, they can move select parts of their IT enterprise into the cloud to establish hybrid architectures. The application of service-orientation can directly enhance the design quality of cloud-based solutions, especially those using shared services.

There are three main benefits associated with the adoption of cloud computing:

- Reduced Investment and Proportional Costs
- Increased Scalability
- Increased Availability and Reliability

All three benefits lead to the potential of establishing highly agile and resilient environments that can increase the potential of realizing service-oriented computing goals. This is why the mainstream emergence of cloud computing is considered a primary driver of what constitutes next generation SOA.

At the same time, there are risks and challenges that are inherent to clouds and cloud-based technology that need to be factored in when considering their usage. These concerns include the following:

- Increased Security Vulnerabilities
- Reduced Operational Governance Control
- Limited Portability Between Cloud Providers
- Multi-Regional Compliance and Legal Issues

Some of these risks are of particular concern to service-oriented ecosystems that rely on shared and composable services.

Appendix C provides detailed descriptions of the aforementioned benefits, risks, and challenges.

API Management

Some shared services are used predominantly in public domains to provide crossover functions, such as adding content from multiple social media accounts or public data services, mashing content with maps, and embedding videos. To facilitate these types of high-traffic interactions, commercial-grade APIs are created, typically based on mainstream Web technologies such as SOAP, REST, and JavaScript.

A number of vendors offer API management solutions for these types of shared services that include API definition, billing, intermediation, security, analytics, and auditing. Clouds can host these offerings to help the organizations that publish APIs create sustainable platforms without significant investment.

Embedding third-party APIs into solutions or Web sites often does not require much effort, and APIs from different providers can be mashed together to create interesting content and innovative linkages. Web-based API management tools and platforms can assist with the management of both in-house and external third-party services that are part of service-oriented solutions.

Model-Driven Software Design

In the late 1990s, when object-orientation was the predominant software development paradigm, many thought leaders promoted model-driven architecture (MDA) as a means of modeling the relevant parts of a business domain that were to be automated. The Unified Markup Language (UML) could then be used to generate large portions of executable software logic from those models. However, this approach failed to become widely adopted.

Just like MDA, Model-Driven Software Design (MDSD) is an approach that focuses on the model and the generation of corresponding executable logic. The difference is primarily that MDSD is less complex and tackles a much narrower scope of solution design than MDA. It addresses distinct parts of the overall architecture, namely those mostly suitable for modeling. MDSD practices can be applied to align business logic with technical service contract design. It is essential to have a business-readable and designable service contract that includes capabilities, faults, message interaction patterns, service-level agreement (SLA) support, and other functional and non-functional features.

A prime SOA example is the automated generation of standardized service contracts and chosen parts of the distinct technology representation based on a developed contract design language that the business sector can understand, without requiring IT expertise. The ultimate goal of MDSD is to establish a service factory in order to foster more flexible and automated software development, where creativity is transferred from individual software artifacts to the centrally governed code generators. This approach increases reusability and reduces maintenance efforts, as design changes can be applied at a central location.

Semantic Web

Semantic Web technologies enable disparate systems to communicate in the same language without having to necessarily implement standard messaging definitions. Semantic computing is a natural extension to SOA. This form of computing represents a "universal decoder" that allows software, services, and even specialized appliances to seamlessly interoperate.

A common language or vocabulary can be established and terms defined through this language have the same meaning regardless of how they are used. Services are then typically defined as self-contained, self-describing, and semantically marked-up resources that can be published, discovered, and executed via automation.

Semantic Web technology describes artifacts and their properties and relationships using language that can be processed by machines to create metadata that is applicable at different levels in an SOA ecosystem.

The following are three primary semantic Web technologies:

- *Resource Description Framework (RDF)* – a metadata modeling standard that uses entity-relationship and class diagram approaches to express relationships captured within statements

- *Ontology Web Language (OWL)* – a knowledge representation language used for the formal definition of ontologies that can express deep relationships and properties

- *Simple Knowledge Organization System (SKOS)* – a formal language built on RDF to enable vocabularies to be published for the Semantic Web

Semantics can accurately describe services, the data exchanged and state data shared or deferred by services, service capabilities and compositions, and IT resources used or shared by services. Semantic Web technologies can be positioned within service-oriented architecture to enhance communication intelligence and to abstract semantic metadata from the actual, individual service architectures.

Business Process Management

Business process management (BPM) systems are used as a tool set in combination with a given methodology to model and execute business processes. Process steps are subsequently automated via services as functional building blocks that interact with each other, as well as with end-users and external systems. The Business Process Model and Notation (BPMN) is the formal notation of BPM. Process model artifacts from version BPMN 2.0 onward have the potential to be modeled as well as executed, via the transformation of the model into code.

A primary goal of BPM is to view each business process not just as a business function, but as a potential cross-functional initiative. Locally identified services and processes can be designed in alignment with the universally defined SOA principles to support participation in enterprise-wide processes. Consequently, the core value-adding chains that reflect the ultimate business goals can be found at the highest level of a process chain. If value chains drive BPM efforts, each improvement on a local level can be mapped to enterprise business goals to identify areas of improvement on the macro level, such as maximization of profit, quality improvement, and customer satisfaction.

Composition and Orchestration

A variety of established technologies exist in support of hosting and executing runtime, task-centric service composition logic, as well as more complex and often longer-running orchestration logic. Traditional middleware platforms, such as those provided by enterprise service bus (ESB) products, are generally inherently equipped with process engines, monitoring agents, state deferral mechanisms, and other features that support the carrying out and administering of interactions between composed services.

Several notable industry technologies are commonly used in conjunction with such middleware, including the following:

- *Business Process Execution Language (BPEL)* – used to programmatically express business process logic for unit-based orchestration, invocation of service calls, and with the support of compensation routines

- *Event-Driven Process Chain (EPC)* – a resource-intensive approach to creating high-level models based on events, execute functions, and invocation gateways and rules for decisions and resources

- *Business Process Model and Notation (BPMN)* – provides a user-friendly notation and establishes a standardized bridge for the gap between the design and the implementation of a business process

- *Adaptive Case Management (ACM)* – an alternative approach that does not dictate the exact process logic flow, in support of adaptive, unstructured business processes that cannot be easily formalized in a process model notation

The choice of hosting platform, industry technologies, and modeling tools used for service composition and orchestration is critical to the success of service-oriented architecture implementations. This is due to the core emphasis of service-orientation on delivering highly composable services.

Master Data Management

A system landscape can become fragmented from the implementation of point solutions by different organizational units throughout the enterprise. The fragmentation of data across systems reduces data quality and increases difficulty in day-to-day changes, producing inconsistencies across the system. Master data management (MDM) provides a cohesive means of maintaining datasets that are used across a system.

Resolving system fragmentation increases data quality and improves data maintenance, as any changes that are made to data can be managed for consistency and interoperability. An MDM system can be used to resolve semantic incompatibilities, declare constraints, check data flow integrity, and audit, cleanse, and recycle rejected records, as well as consolidate and federate referential data.

MDM handles the creation and maintenance of the basic data objects or entities that most organizations require to conduct business, such as "customer". These basic data objects are used within business processes to support the creation and referential integrity of transactional entities that manage cash flow or products. Transactional entities are characterized by their ability to span functional boundaries and change state frequently throughout the lifecycle of a process.

Many vendors offer MDM platforms that not only centralize and manage master data records, but also come with a comprehensive and customizable set of service APIs. This feature enables enterprises to reach the goal of cohesive MDM through a modern platform that includes a set of related capabilities. As a result, MDM is becoming increasingly important to the development of data-centric services.

Business Rule Engines

A business rule engine (BRE) is a specialized software program that contains customizable, conditional logic that enables it to implement and execute a wide range of business rules. Centralization of business rules using a BRE allows this segment of business logic to exist and be administered and evolved independently from solution and service logic.

Business rules can represent business or governance policies, workflow decision points, or actions in response to business events. Depending on the nature and complexity of a given business rule, some service capability invocations may be reduced to a single call of a BRE.

The evolution of BREs has focused on collaborating synergistically with ESB and BPM technologies to produce a line of pervasive and lightweight BRE technologies.

Social Network Technologies

The advent of social media sparked the creation of new Web technology that enhances creativity, collaboration, and Web functionality. This has led to the emergence of Web culture communities and hosted services such as social networking sites, video-sharing sites, wikis, and blogs. Such services can be designed to seek interconnections and consume and remix data from multiple sources.

The extent to which services that encapsulate this type of functionality can make their way into service-oriented architectures depends on how relevant the data that they process is to serving an organization's business needs. As discussed later in this chapter, the tools and technologies that have emerged in support of Big Data can enable shared services to process and even interpret this social media data to optimize or dictate certain runtime behaviors.

Mobile Computing

Mobile applications are heavily used to supplement business-to-consumer (B2C) interactions for a wide range of applications and solution logic. The concept of specialized helpers for every imaginable task and entertainment option resulted in the creation of "app" stores from where users can install new functionality on mobile devices with a single tap.

Mobile devices provide alternative channels for exposing existing services to new potential service consumers. Consequently, they have introduced user-interfaces with different resolutions and screen sizes, as well as different interaction mechanisms (touchscreen, pen, keyboard, etc.). While existing service logic can be shared and extended to support the use of mobile devices, user-interface and communication-related limitations typically impose the need for further processing and presentation logic customization.

On the server side, communicating with mobile apps often requires a new channel-specific technical layer on top of existing service layers. Mobile applications are considered to be first-class citizens that must be able to trigger and fully participate in automated business processes. Enabling users to provide input through mobile applications as part of their business process activities can introduce the need for dedicated services that abstract the logic required to cope with the distinct requirements and demands of mobile computing.

Agent-Driven Architecture

Services that interact with each other typically exchange messages which can be intercepted and processed by service agents that subsequently take action using an event-driven software architecture. Alternatively, service agents can generate messages or other forms of communication via internally driven events.

Although agent-driven software design is by no means a recent innovation, their specific usage in conjunction with service-orientation principles needs to be carefully assessed to ensure that the separation of logic between service agents and services is appropriate, and also to identify opportunities to utilize service agents in support of increasing the effectiveness and agility of enterprise solutions.

Service agents do not have published APIs. They are event-driven, which means that their logic is automatically invoked upon the occurrence of certain runtime events. They are developed and deployed for many specialized purposes, including user authentication, message conversion and routing, security policy checking, and other runtime monitoring and management functions. The type of development platform and functionality selected determines whether a service agent is called a listener, filter, interceptor, or handler.

The global nature of the Internet makes keeping the unique functionality of each service that is added, advertised, and articulated in local/remote and private/public service inventories very challenging. In this context, service agents are important in preserving service functionality so as to promote dynamic service interaction and orchestration. A variety of approaches and product offerings that guarantee the efficacy of service agents in fulfilling the composition of services at runtime are available.

Semantic technologies are used by agents to perform completely automated composition and can play a role in ensuring that service composition is meaningful and dynamic. Service composition can be performed dynamically through agent collaboration without pre-defining abstract plans. Agent technology offers a range of mechanisms to formally express and use richer semantic annotations.

Event-Driven Architecture and Complex Event Processing

Event-driven architecture (EDA) is specifically related to the processing and routing of asynchronous events, which is based on the concept of posting events to a central processing facility that can make decisions on how to route or process them. The primary difference between EDA and SOA lies in EDA's strictly asynchronous nature.

Most ESBs provide event-processing capabilities that are typically derived from existing features, such as asynchronous messaging, transformation, content-based routing, business rules, and publish/subscribe mechanisms. Some vendors offer distinct complex event processing (CEP) facilities that incorporate BPM, business rules, and transaction functionality.

An event ontology is a formal specification within a shared domain that defines the process for sharing realtime events between components. In the context of event-driven architecture, an event ontology manages change data capture (CDC) and complex event-driven processing. CDC capabilities can perform scheduled, on-demand, or full updates and reloads of data, as well as allow for continuous loads to the data warehouse that can detect changes on different data sources in order to pull or push data.

While the importance of loose coupling in SOA is well emphasized, EDA takes it a step further. An event in an EDA is generated by an event source and sent to the processing middleware, which determines the functionality to be triggered afterwards. In SOA, on the other hand, a concrete service call would have had to be made. For this reason, the term "decoupling" and not "loose coupling" is used in relation to EDA, as an "event-driven application" consumes processes and generates events in a decoupled fashion. The processing middleware accepts the events, evaluates the contents, and checks the contents against a set of criteria where applicable, before notifying interested consumers using a publish/subscribe model.

The discipline of complex event processing differs from traditional processing mechanisms that are based on queues or databases in how CEP also involves caches that allow for complex correlations of different events, including over-extended time horizons. This is becoming increasingly important in stream processing, with the emergence of SQL-type, stream-based query languages. Rule engines are typically used to define and execute all of the rules associated with event routing, processing, and correlation.

SOA and EDA are complementary to one another, and when applied in combination permit the creation of on-demand applications with significant business benefits. A noteworthy consideration, however, is the governance of events, including the semantic descriptions behind events. While services inherently express capabilities through a contract which may or may not include non-functional requirements, events are singular data structures.

Business Intelligence

The emergence of SOA has forced change across many disciplines, not the least of which is business intelligence (BI). This umbrella term encompasses the tools that can be used for consolidated analytics in business user-friendly dashboards. These tools are a crucial building block of next generation SOA, since they allow enterprise architecture models and business process models to be linked with both historical and realtime data.

The desired outcome of a BI initiative is an enterprise architecture management dashboard that allows holistic insights into both the static and dynamic aspects of the IT landscape and their impact on the critical core business processes. The ability to monitor service executions enables instantaneous feedback to be provided on the nature and level of business transactions.

A typical characteristic of contemporary BI is a time delay that results from the complexity of the consolidation and analysis operations that are generally run in nightly batches and performed to assist in the evaluation of critical KPIs. Alternatively, business activity monitoring (BAM) is a viable foundation for next generation BI that implements direct monitoring of running process instances to gain immediate insight into critical events in business processes.

Determining the connection between BI and business processes is a considerable challenge for enterprises that want to identify and optimize core value chains. Once successful, however, integration of these two disciplines can offer insight of greater clarity into the inner workings of an enterprise than could be accomplished by process simulation.

Decision-makers are promptly enabled to react to unpredictable scenarios by, for example, initiating other processes or actions. BI itself can trigger many actions automatically in realtime without human involvement when certain patterns are discovered in business processes.

Enterprises use software that tracks critical business KPIs, such as the amount of orders per day, and SLAs for tracking the downtime of important subsystems. A synergistic relationship between SOA and BI tools can help to streamline the complexity and heterogeneity of IT infrastructures and the application landscape that would otherwise introduce complications. The core disciplines of next generation BI insight-driven business processes include direct BI process coupling, automated reporting, alerting, and dashboard updates. Various aspects of SOA effectively lend themselves to facilitating BI activities. In the field of predictive analytics, CEP and intelligent rule engines can be used to determine and create adaptive recommendations that predict areas for action. For business process analysis, the SOA infrastructure generates large amounts of runtime data that BI can condense into meaningful information about realtime process behavior.

Enterprise Information Integration and Extract-Transform-Load

BI components that are anticipated to achieve integration into SOA solutions include enterprise information integration (EII) and extract-transform-load (ETL) processes. EII is a metadata-driven infrastructure that supports access to multiple data sources through data virtualization, providing a complete view of data as if it exists in a single, relational database with read and write SQL. The result is an enterprise-wide view of data that forms a reusable framework for information access to address the problems involved in integrating spaghetti architectures while creating a data layer for SOA services.

EII is able to federate SQL queries as needed. Web-based services such as those that provide stock quotes and weather updates can provide data on-demand, information that can also be provided through browsers. When combining data from Web sources with operational data, users are provided with a more unified view of disparate information.

ETLs are the fundamental processes of moving data (usually via bulk transfer) from source systems to target fact and dimension tables in data warehouses, and can be executed to load source databases, staging tables, operational data stores, data warehouses, and data marts. Using an open-source ETL package is more cost-effective than hand-crafting an in-house ETL. Web-based service adapters can be used to provide

Web service interfaces to application systems, database systems, and platform systems, and can also transform non-XML formats into XML formats.

Big Data

Data volumes have been rapidly increasing as the result of a host of different factors, such as mobile computing and social networking. This high rate of growth is demanding that businesses become proficient at the near-realtime processing and interpretation of data originating from heterogeneous sources, in order to remain competitive. Data that is maintained in well-defined formats in corporate data stores is no longer sufficient. Organizations must tap into new, unstructured datasets in order to gain valuable insights about service consumer behaviors, market trends, and customer preferences in the domain of Big Data.

Big Data is defined as a field dedicated to the analysis, processing, and storage of large collections of data that frequently originate from disparate sources. Big Data solutions and practices are typically required when traditional data analysis, processing, and storage technologies and techniques are insufficient. Specifically, Big Data addresses distinct requirements, such as the combining of multiple unrelated datasets, processing of large amounts of unstructured data, and harvesting of hidden information, in a time-sensitive manner.

Companies have adopted two distinct approaches in an attempt to manage Big Data: BI reporting and realtime analytics. BI reporting is not too different from traditional reporting methods except in the tools and techniques that are used to collect, store, interpret, and present data. The same is true of realtime analytics, which makes use of an advanced set of tools to handle structured, semi-structured, and unstructured data. The heterogeneous nature of Big Data requires the data to be interpreted and handled in a consistent manner, which can be performed by a service that is specifically built to deliver data to a variety of destinations. Consumers of these services are able to process data regardless of its source, syntax, or semantic meaning.

Service-enabled middleware can help to streamline the handling of large volumes of data and transactions, while EDA can be leveraged to post and process all new events coming from various data sources. BREs can be utilized to take immediate action based on specific scenario conditions, and BPM tools can be implemented to quickly modify business processes in response to changing conditions.

When these technologies become a part of the enterprise's system environment, SOA can assume a prominent role. Event-based activity monitoring and analytics can be applied to BI scenarios in which asynchronous service interfaces are utilized to capture all essential events. Big Data realtime analytics operations can be exposed as decision services and integrated with appropriate processes and applications to enhance decision-making. Any administrative or supporting services that are created to enable Big Data operations can be exposed to other tools or management consoles to take advantage of any Big Data processes already running in the enterprise.

Big Data and SOA are a natural fit for one another in how Big Data solutions can provide an enterprise with valuable insights that can become actionable upon synergistic collaboration with SOA.

Through the application of service-enabling Big Data processes, organizations can reach the next level of competitive differentiation and agility, namely realtime analytics. Data about customer interactions, system health, and unexpected conditions from various data sources is collected throughout the enterprise. Multiple disjointed events reach corporate systems simultaneously. Businesses that can process and interpret the mass of heterogeneous data to detect trends and react instantaneously to resolve customer issues will rise above the competition. There is nothing more gratifying to customers than having their concerns addressed before having to call customer support.

The ability to expose Big Data-based events, decision-making, and administrative services across an entire supply chain enables an IT enterprise to take advantage of realtime insights on a potentially global scale. While Big Data may prove to be the lifeblood of an organization, SOA can become the arteries that sustain the organization's IT enterprise.

Chapter 6

A Look at Service-Driven Industry Models

The Enterprise Service Model

The Virtual Enterprise Model

The Capacity Trader Model

The Enhanced Wholesaler Model

The Price Comparator Model

The Content Provider Model

The Job Market Model

The Global Trader Model

The convergences of modern SOA practices with service technologies have been creating opportunities to form new business relationships and operational models. Intended to inspire the construction of custom models for organizations in any industry, a series of innovative models that highlight the potential of next generation SOA is explored in this chapter.

The Enterprise Service Model

The enterprise service model combines capability, business processes, organization models, and data models into a single unified view of the business and its development priorities. All of the industry models described in the upcoming sections rely on the participation of one or more service-enabled organizations and, correspondingly, the existence of one or more enterprise service models.

As a conceptual simulation of how an enterprise operates, this type of model can be applied to any organization. Developing such a model for an enterprise is valuable because any of the services contained therein can be delivered directly by IT assets using automated business processes or delivered as transactional units of business logic.

A unified model defines a physical inventory of services for implementation as IT assets and provides a common language that can be used by both business and IT professionals to better understand the other's priorities, needs, and expectations. This alignment of IT and business encourages the development of IT solutions that can map accurately to and better support business processes, which in turn enhances business efficiency in the ability to capitalize on new opportunities and respond to new challenges. While next generation service-oriented enterprises already tend to use some service technologies to optimize business operations and achieve strategic business goals, new business opportunities can uniquely drive IT to embrace other, more diverse service technologies in an effort to leverage best-of-breed offerings.

Enterprises can have a large inventory of shared and deployed business services ranging from basic business transactions to automated, complex, or long-running business processes. With a well-defined enterprise service model of primary business activities, enterprises can prioritize solutions and leverage business models that provide the foundation for reusable services. Solutions might include discovering new potential business partners, comparing vendor deals, and on-boarding new vendors. A well-defined service model offers a service consumer-service provider approach to conducting business between operating units within the enterprise and between the enterprise and its business partners.

Next generation SOA allows for the creation of a complete ecosystem that connects and supports both business and IT, providing full integration of business objectives, operations and processes, standards, rules, governance, and IT infrastructure and assets. Enterprises can base their information models on industry standards to facilitate the interoperability of custom services with business partners and other third parties.

The first step in developing an enterprise service model is to define high-level services that are then decomposed into progressively finer-grained services representing business activities, processes, and tasks. The service inventory contains all of the services from the service model that have been physically realized as IT assets. These services can be purchased commercially, developed internally, or provided by third parties.

The service approach readily identifies repeated tasks that are common to multiple different business units and business processes. Reusable services that perform these repeated tasks should undergo automation only once to avoid unnecessary duplication and simplify the overall complexity of the IT domain. Some utility-centric services, such as those that provide security, monitoring, and reporting-related processing, are highly reusable across all business domains. Since the physical services in the inventory mirror business processes, activities, and tasks, monitoring their execution can provide a real-time picture of how the enterprise is performing relative to its business targets, which is generally unachievable with commercial application packages.

The Virtual Enterprise Model

In the virtual enterprise model, companies join together in a loose federation to compete with major players in the same industry. The virtualization of a collective enterprise enables the member enterprises to collaborate on a specific business opportunity, and affords them the freedom of rapidly disbanding with relatively little impact on the individual enterprise. A virtual enterprise is a dynamic consortium of small and medium enterprises (SMEs) that have agreed to combine efforts to create a joint product or to bid for a major contract. Large corporations may also form consortia for large-scale projects. By leveraging cloud computing advances, virtual enterprises can become indistinguishable from physical enterprises as far as externally-facing customers and users are concerned, since they typically have minimal physical presence and often little to no in-house infrastructure.

Members of the consortium may compete with each other outside the agreed scope of the virtual enterprise's area of operations. This model allows small businesses to compete for major contracts or create products of higher complexity. Each consortium member contributes their existing skills and capabilities, and benefits from the ability to collectively achieve a result that none could accomplish individually. Opportunities, profits, and risks are shared across the consortium.

In this highly flexible model, virtual enterprises can form, expand, contract, and dissolve rapidly and inexpensively to meet market opportunities after establishing collective trust. Effective governance is required to coordinate the efforts of individual consortium members, and SOA technology can enable the integration of supply chains across the entire virtual enterprise. Service contracts and interfaces provide for clear communication between consortium members, while facilitating the addition and withdrawal of members to and from the virtual enterprise without requiring major changes to their infrastructure.

Many cross-enterprise business processes can be automated. The monitoring and reporting of automated processes and transactional service executions provides consortium members with accurate, realtime data on the state and operations of the virtual enterprise. This business model is mainly relevant for the manufacturing, distribution, retail, and service industries, as well as business opportunities provided by one-time events like the Super Bowl or Olympic Games.

A simple but promising variant of this approach would be an entrepreneurial organization whose business model is to act as a virtual holding company. A virtual holding company creates and manages virtual enterprises without being an active participant in the manufacturing of products or service offerings.

The Capacity Trader Model

In the capacity trader model, IT capacity is sold to customers as a commodity in a cloud computing environment. Parties with spare IT capacity sell to clients who require extra capacity. IT capacity traders buy and sell IT capacity to commercial users. Typically, these users operate in a different time zone and will use the purchased capacity outside of the capacity trader's normal working hours. Capacity may also become available as the result of an oversized data center, a reduction in processing demand caused by business losses, or an overt business strategy.

Some organizations use the capacity trader model as a foundational business model to create IT capacity for sale to commercial users, while others offer capacity brokerage services and sign up multiple small capacity traders to create a high-capacity bundle that can be marketed at a premium. The capacity trader model is the 21st-century equivalent of the data center of the 1970s. Amazon.com, Inc. was the first company to sell its extra computing capacity, and many large computer companies have adopted this model to follow in its footsteps.

The Enhanced Wholesaler Model

According to the enhanced wholesaler model, the high speeds at which service-oriented automation enables wholesalers to receive contract bids from suppliers allow the wholesalers to respond more dynamically to demand, reduce, or even eliminate storage costs, and maximize profits. Traditional wholesalers buy products from multiple suppliers to sell to individual customers. The enhanced wholesaler model relies on one-stop shopping to meet customer needs for a range of products and reduce unit costs by purchasing large quantities from individual suppliers.

This model is in sharp contrast to the base wholesaler business model, where the wholesaler purchases goods or services from suppliers to sells them to customers at a profit. The enhanced wholesaler can secure the best deals from many potential bidders, and, if necessary, combine their offerings to meet each customer's requirements. It can further charge a commission for locating and introducing customers to suppliers.

Service technology improves on the enhanced wholesaler model by enabling the wholesaler to expand its network of suppliers and customers. The creation, enforcing, and monitoring of formal contracts helps the wholesaler maintain multiple business relationships, while the global nature of the Web has increased opportunities to trade over great distances. Warehousing costs may be eliminated in some cases by using drop shipping, where the manufacturer delivers the goods directly to the end user.

The Price Comparator Model

The price comparator model is where a commercial organization compares the bids of multiple competing suppliers to find the best possible deal for a potential customer. Price comparators perform the service of requesting and managing quotes from multiple competing companies for common commodities, such as insurance, hotel accommodation, or rental cars. Profits are based on commission per sale and a commission fee is typically charged to the successful vendor.

In many cases, price comparators give potential customers access to multiple quotes for common goods or services through a dedicated Web site. The visitor first enters their details to contact multiple potential vendors for different quotes before selecting a preferred option based on a combination of features and price and making the purchase. In such instances, the price comparison site takes a commission on the purchase.

Unlike enhanced wholesalers, price comparators never own the products they market, but simply act as intermediaries between the buyer and seller. Setup costs are low, but a substantial investment is required for advertising if the site targets private customers, as there is massive competition in some industries. Service technology enables price comparison sites to contact many potential providers in parallel and then rank and display their offerings in realtime. Financial details of the purchase transaction can be exchanged securely and promptly. This model adapts to any industry that markets goods and services to the general public.

The Content Provider Model

Content providers create information feeds containing textual, pictorial, and multimedia data for service consumers to access. Increasing availability of high-bandwidth communications has resulted in significant growth in the amount of electronically transmitted information, including items like sports feeds and movies. A content provider supplies information feeds to information aggregator organizations, such as telephone companies, the press, and commercial Web sites, that make such content available to customers for a direct fee or through funding from advertisers. The owner of an electronic asset can make that content available to a wide number of information integrators.

Piracy can be an issue, especially in the software and entertainment industries. Services provide a secure channel between the content provider and the content aggregator, while service monitoring can be implemented to automate the billing process and provide an audit trail. Multimedia, software, and e-books currently dominate the content provider model. Some content providers deal directly with retail customers rather than through content aggregators.

The Job Market Model

In the job market model, enterprises locate and hire contractors that possess the skills suitable for specific tasks. In recent years, the job market has become more dynamic and fluid. It was once common for new graduates to have a single career specialization and to even be employed by the same company their entire working life, while graduates nowadays are generally expected to have multiple specializations, employers, and careers. Increasingly more professionals are working as short-term contractors rather than as long-term employees. The job market model is a specialized form of the employment agency that maintains a database of contractors with different skill sets and qualifications to meet the specific needs of employers.

The principal differences between the job market model's contractor job center and an employment agency is that the positions filled are short-term rather than permanent, and that the contractors may be any combination of individuals and subcontracting companies. Using a contractor job center allows both the employer and the contractor to be part of a global marketplace without having to invest in infrastructure enterprises, which can reduce per-capita employment overheads and physical infrastructure costs. Business flexibility and agility can also be increased through the use of subcontractors rather than full-time employees. The number of contractors can be rapidly scaled up or down to dynamically meet business demands.

The increasing availability of high-bandwidth connectivity will enable many employees to work from rural or suburban locations, requiring a change in culture for many traditional businesses which will now need to employ individuals that they may never physically meet. Services provide a secure and precise means of communication between all parties. Service contracts provide information about the timing of requests and responses, and service interfaces allow software developers to remotely test and integrate systems code.

Service technology can automate the bidding process for each opportunity. The SOA infrastructure can use the agency to notify individuals of all of the opportunities for which they are qualified via a variety of channels, such as e-mail or instant messaging.

Most administrative processes can be automated to reduce setup and operating costs for the agency. While particularly appropriate for IT consultants, this model is likely the future of work for many professionals and administrative staff in many industries, who will either work from home or for small businesses. Contractor agents can be considered to be subcontractors in their own right. In addition to providing prospective employers with a list of candidates, they also employ the contractors themselves and are responsible for their performance. An alternative approach is to create a consultant market in which individuals or organizations bid against each other for specific contract opportunities. In this model, the contractor agency manages the bidding and vetoes or rates the bidder.

The Global Trader Model

The global trader model allows for an international marketing reach. While the Internet has certainly been successful at increasing the globalization of trade, some inhibitors still remain. The key issues involve trust, differences in commercial law and enforcement of those laws, and non-existent international standards.

Issues of trust exist whenever two organizations do business with one another. While Web standards help to provide secure communications, proof of identity, and an audit trail, they do not provide the ability to guarantee that each organization will fulfill contractual promises or that the quality of goods delivered or services performed will be satisfactory. This is especially problematic when the two organizations operate in different countries.

Differences in commercial laws and law enforcement are a problem for both enterprises and governments. Generally, enterprises cannot be confident that a foreign supplier's government will take appropriate action if that supplier breaches a business contract. Government bodies, especially those involved in customs and taxation, want to be sure that they are kept well-informed of all transfers of goods and chargeable services into and from their countries, which can be difficult to achieve if the transfers are performed electronically.

Few industries have standards that are truly international, and many countries handle business accounting and taxation quite differently. Addresses, for example, can take many different forms around the globe, while certain countries do not use a social security number or other unique identifier for each citizen. Two types of organizations known as industry watchdogs and guarantors have been established to address various inhibitors to global trade.

Industry Watchdogs

An industry watchdog is a trusted third party that has the authority to certify companies that have met a recognized set of performance standards. This helps to promote free trade by reducing the risk of dealing with unknown suppliers. On the other hand, certification is not a guarantee of quality, and certified companies that commit a breach of trust may lose their status. In some countries, the capacity of watchdogs is limited to the regulation of companies within borders, while most regulators in the United States can only operate within an individual state.

Guarantors

Guarantors use the insurance model to provide more active protection of individual business transactions, ensuring that each of the parties involved in a specific single contract fulfills its obligations. A guarantor acts as an intermediary for commercial business transactions and reimburses the customer in the event that the supplier fails to meet contractual obligations. A common method of reimbursement is for the guarantor to act as an escrow account, taking payment from the customer but not paying the supplier until the goods or services have been provided.

The guarantor can profit from this approach by earning interest on the fees held in escrow. However, reimbursing customers for high-value business transactions gone awry without a relatively high volume of business can present a risk, and excessive reimbursement can damage the guarantor's profitability. A relationship of trust with both clients and suppliers first needs to be established in order for the escrow model to succeed. A standalone retail transaction insurer could also use this business model.

Chapter 7

A Case Study

Systems Landscape

New Marketing Strategy

Corporate Culture

Vehicle Maintenance

The Billing System

Strategic Considerations

Cloud Adoption

New Reference Architecture

The Customer Profile Process

New Service Technology

The SOA Governance
Program Office

The Enterprise
Architecture Board

A Transformed Enterprise

Rent Your Legacy Car (RYLC) is a publicly owned car leasing company that was founded in the late 1990s. The company offers a wide variety of quality vehicles for short- or long-term lease to the southwestern United States. In recent years, RYLC was unable to adapt to changes in market conditions and deliver new system capabilities more readily than the competition, falling behind in sales. The company must now regain lost market share or face dire consequences.

RYLC's board of directors has become increasingly concerned about hostile takeovers that have targeted other similar-sized companies in the industry. Rumors suggest that RYLC is next. The seven-person board consists of three outside members, one of whom represents a hedge fund with a 32% stake. Also on the board is the chairman and three senior vice presidents who respectively chair the steering, audit, and human resources committees that support strategic planning.

The board recently hired a new CIO named Robert. A 25-year veteran in the industry, Robert has managed major SOA projects in a CTO role at two other retail corporations, helping both companies make significant gains in profitability and market share that further increased their respective stock prices. RYLC's CEO, Jesse, was instrumental in recruiting Robert to come on board. Jesse considers Robert to be an asset that can help him improve the company's precarious position and address some further business culture concerns.

Days after being hired, Robert and the board establish a five-year plan to move from seventh to third place in net revenue among ten of its key competitors, along with other ambitious financial and stock metrics. Robert believes a large SOA environment integrated with cloud infrastructure will equip RYLC with a service-driven and highly scalable IT enterprise.

RYLC can position its services for aggressive growth while significantly cutting costs and time to market, as shown in Table 7.1.

Jane, the senior vice president who also chairs the audit committee, supports this initiative. However, she stipulates that Robert must maintain quarterly metrics that include comparative measures of uptime percentage, security intrusion counts, mean-times between failures, mean-times to repair high severity tickets, and the average utilization rates of servers and storage devices.

Strategic Goals	Functions	RYLC (Present)	RYLC (Future)
increase speed and flexibility	test provisioning	weeks	minutes
	change management	months	hours
	release management	weeks	minutes
reduce costs	server/storage utilization	10% - 20%	70% - 90%
	payback period	years	months

Table 7.1
A summary of RYLC's five-year plan outlines savings in application development that are obtained from making use of the cloud. The use of cloud-based IT resources is a core component of this strategy.

The board supports the bold service technologies strategy with the understanding that the savings realized can be put into marketing, talent acquisition, mergers, expansion, and shareholder rewards. Robert is approved to restructure RYLC with a new team and new service technologies so long as returns on investment are realized on schedule. He makes a further request for RYLC to compile forced employee rankings in order to assess their performance, so as to better understand the capabilities of the existing employees. Robert spends time visiting and assessing each department and branch office for the first month, observing the social dynamics, tools, quality of data, and customer issues of each team.

The news that Robert has become RYLC's new CIO is met with mixed reception. There is skepticism in the business community, which carries over into business cable channels. Institutional owners and funds show uncertainty and doubt through heavy selling. The month of March experiences a stock equity valuation slippage of seven million dollars. A month after his arrival, Robert briefs the board on his assessment of the company's current state.

Systems Landscape

Robert asks the lead enterprise architect, Andrew, and his team to analyze RYLC's current system landscape for problems. They discover that RYLC has a chaotic application landscape that had grown organically over the past two decades to produce a confusing web of mainframe, client, and EAI architectures. Multiple batch runs are performed to compensate for the lack of functional integration. RYLC has dwindling expertise due to outdated technology and high employee turnover, and lacks centralized user and rights management, as well as tight controls and governance over master data.

The car rental application (CRA) is the newest member of the system landscape. It exists as a client-server application that links the individual branch offices with the head office using a star topology. The IT staff has continually expanded this application to meet new demands over the past few years, introducing J2EE architecture along with other frameworks that include open-source and vendor products. For example, an XML file sent via a Web service interface performs batch reconciliation with all of the branch offices twice a day.

Each system implements its own application-specific user management, including authorization and authentication. After introducing the J2EE car rental application, RYLC decided to pursue a central identity management solution to reduce administrative costs.

An EJB application interfaces with branch offices via RMI and with other applications using batch interfaces, while an EAI solution is used to integrate other applications for the batch interchange. Any errors that occur are rectified manually, and isolating the cause of an error is often time-consuming.

Customer invoices are processed using a 30-year old COBOL system that runs on a mainframe. Interfaces with the other systems have been in operation for a long time and can only be maintained by two older employees who are nearing retirement. The invoicing system also uses an off-the-shelf car rental application that manages car purchases, repairs, and sales. This standalone application, along with a proprietary database, provides XML interfaces and a Procedural Language/Structured Query Language (PL/SQL) API for data interchange.

The legacy environment also houses two standard CRM solutions that are used primarily for customer history and marketing campaigns. Customer data can be maintained simultaneously in both CRM systems, depending on the user role and system usage. Data reconciliations are performed daily, and any semblance of data governance is conspicuously absent. Master data resides in a system that is different from the one used for site administration.

RYLC cannot automate workflows and processes due to inadequate system integration capabilities and the presence of multiple interfaces and protocols in the systems environment. Online processing with high uptime is not possible due to asynchronous integration from nightly batch runs. Security is often implemented within individual systems and can only be approved by the IT department. The company's systems landscape does not possess any comprehensive single sign-on (SSO) capabilities.

Data that varies widely in quality across applications is stored at different locations and is even duplicated in some cases. The process for defining access to the customer data is carried out on a variety of isolated applications by staff who only rely on their memory, resulting in a low degree of standardization. In short, RYLC's ecosystem is inundated with legacy applications and a myriad of uncontrolled batch connections to neighboring systems.

The board is not surprised by Robert's assessment, as management has been attempting to resolve these problems for years. A data warehouse is established in order for the company to be able to calculate customer sales trends and extract data from all of the various systems. To improve data quality, a team of students is hired to manually perform maintenance operations. However, taking these measures does not solve RYLC's immediate problems as the architecture is too inflexible.

New Marketing Strategy

As part of an ambitious strategy to regain market share, Robert plans to introduce additional sales channels through e-commerce, since the company's direct sales channels are currently only found at central travel hubs like airports, train stations, and ports. He also intends to improve the company's quality of service through heightened control over each rental vehicle's condition and tighter maintenance cycles for faster turnaround times.

In addition to establishing new sales channels, Robert suggests that the company should also focus on taking over smaller competitors in order to further increase market share. A service-oriented cloud will be used for operational support and scaling, and an ESB will be implemented to orchestrate an inventory of services. Customer service support is scheduled to be offshored to Kuala Lumpur, Malaysia in six months. Further growth will be achieved through international franchising opportunities and expansion of existing operations, with a strategic acquisition in Dallas, Texas. Robert also asks the vice president of business development, Mary, to begin the process of establishing virtual offices in Singapore, Kuala Lumpur, and Bandung, while also looking for potential business partners in these regions.

After consulting with several functionality experts, Robert proposes that RYLC develop and roll out a new strategy aimed at improving customer service. A key part of the strategy is introducing a high-quality service that would be able to guarantee customers a rental car at their requested collection point within one hour. The car can be dropped off anywhere by the customer for pick-up by an RYLC representative at no extra charge. Customers that pick up or return their vehicles at a rental location themselves would receive a discount.

The marketing plan that Robert proposes to the board indicates that the company will transform into a multinational corporation with marketing operations in multiple continents around the globe. Robert asks James, his chief technical officer with 18 years of experience at the company, for an analysis regarding the feasibility of offshoring software development. The plan also involves contracting out for the technical expertise that current employees are lacking, and pairing contingent employees with highly skilled RYLC developers. The company will continue to run with a reduced headcount. Development processes are to be based on an agile development lifecycle, including business intelligence development, while non-regulatory enhancements that are made to existing systems will immediately cease. The IT landscape is to be reorganized into well-defined services.

Robert also intends to allow analysts, developers, architects, and many of the managers to work from home offices using videoconferencing, instant messaging, and other standard forms of modern communication. While this model requires an additional layer of trust and accountability, the savings in commercial office space leasing and commute time for employees are significant. RYLC's marketing reach can be expanded as its physical footprint decreases. The company headquarters will be renovated to include a wing of hotel suites that employees can stay at when needed. Data center resources will be leased and Robert anticipates that the cost savings derived from attrition, internal restructuring, offshoring of IT functions, and market growth can be used to fund RYLC's SOA initiative at least partially. The board agrees to fund the amount that is still remaining.

John, the current CTO, is dubious and insists that the plan is too risky and aggressive. Robert invites him to continue his career elsewhere, with a generous severance package and recognition for his services to the company over the past years. John's termination comes as a surprise to the team and demoralizes many employees, as he was widely liked. The next day, Robert holds his first company-wide meeting to announce that the company's marketing and technology efforts will be aligned to people-first, service-oriented principles from now on. Employees are asked to expect great changes and challenges on the road ahead. He expresses confidence in the team and in the future of the company as a whole. Robert also appoints an interim CTO, asks human resources to begin searching for a new CTO, and establishes a number of employee incentives that include bonuses and stock options.

Corporate Culture

Robert hopes to foster creativity, accountability, and transparency among his employees and encourage authentic communication. Stand-up meetings with the direct subordinates that last 15 minutes are scheduled daily to facilitate ongoing communication. Co-located team members will also take part in stand-ups with their supervisors as a standard best practice for management, with the meetings scheduled for the beginning or end of the day to accommodate offshore support. Each person in attendance is asked to briefly summarize the last 24 hours, state the goals for the next 24 hours, and identify any issues that require immediate attention. One week later, Robert is pleased to see that the stand-up protocol is still being followed by the majority of the teams. RYLC's company culture begins to change.

In the last week of May, Robert holds a two-day strategic planning workshop with key thought leaders from the company's IT and business operating units, including executives, managers, architects, and business analysts. The purpose of this workshop is to come up with innovative ways to enhance RYLC operations by recognizing and responding to business risks and opportunities, improving business performance, and reducing operational costs by increasing productivity and cutting fixed expenses.

The first day is dedicated to identifying business challenges, risks, and opportunities. The marketing director, Jennifer, starts the workshop with an overview of the car rental industry and RYLC's current strategic business plan. Different business executives and IT professionals proceed to give a series of presentations, each describing how their individual business units operate and identifying their main dependencies, issues, opportunities, and inhibitors. Special attention is given to the principal business priorities displayed on the RYLC business heat map (Table 7.2).

The second day of the workshop is dedicated to IT solutions. Robert begins with a description of RYLC's strategic IT roadmap and an overview of various next generation technology capabilities, such as automated business process models and cloud computing. The workshop members are then put into focus groups that are each tasked with addressing a significant issue, problem, or opportunity by coming up with innovative solutions to improve the underlying business processes. Members can move freely between focus group sessions, and a special focus group works on the key strategic areas identified in the RYLC heat map.

Corporate	Fleet Management	Sales and Marketing	Information Technology
product development	vehicle purchasing	advertising and marketing campaigns	application maintenance
corporate acquisitions	vehicle maintenance	customer relations	systems development
profitability and market share	vehicle sales	vehicle delivery and collection	enterprise architecture
location management	cleaning	channel management	data governance
	vehicle availability	billing	

Table 7.2
RYLC's business heat map illustrates the company's main business priorities. Items in darker shaded cells are of higher priority.

The focus groups identify three main issues and two potential opportunities for the company in total. Vehicle maintenance issues are revealed to have a great impact on customer satisfaction, the aging billing system is confirmed to present an unacceptable business risk, and members agree that the complexity of the company's IT system is inhibiting the proposed strategy of growth through mergers and acquisitions. However, vehicle rental volumes can be increased by partnering with other travel comparison Web sites, and IT operational costs can be reduced through the adoption of a cloud computing model.

Vehicle Maintenance

Mounting rental car issues caused by inadequate maintenance are significantly affecting the company's customer satisfaction ratings. RYLC has already lost a number of regular customers who were provided with rental cars that had various defects. Incidents range from an illuminated service warning light and under-inflated tires to low fluid levels and engine failure due to insufficient oil.

The marketing team presents the board with a proposal to modify the in-house rental application by adding an automated check on each rental vehicle's maintenance status, using custom code that follows an event processing approach. A customer's return of a vehicle would generate a business event that would in turn trigger an automated process to determine whether the returned vehicle requires maintenance. The marketing team also presents the option of extending the solution to raise an event whenever a customer is booking a vehicle for an extended period of time, to ensure that the customer is not given a vehicle that requires immediate servicing. Clear separation between rental and fleet maintenance applications can then be achieved to improve the fleet management process. The rental return event can also be used to initiate client invoicing.

The Billing System

The outdated invoicing system runs on a mainframe and is implemented as a custom-developed COBOL application that processes invoices. Interfaces with other systems have been in operation for decades and are currently maintained by two middle-aged employees who are reaching retirement. Maintaining the billing system will be extremely challenging for the remaining employees once these COBOL-savvy programmers leave the company. To resolve this predicament, RYLC decides to move to an open platform and phase out COBOL applications completely.

Proposed options for implementing this plan include:

- hiring more COBOL programmers
- outsourcing maintenance of the billing application
- outsourcing the billing process to an external vendor
- rewriting the billing application in J2EE
- rewriting the billing application as an executable business model
- purchasing a commercial billing system to integrate with RYLC's systems using an ESB

The board decides that, for such a large and potentially expensive project, a high-level focus group of business analysts and architects should first be recruited to identify real-world business requirements for analysis in order to produce the optimal solution. Robert wants a proposal by the middle of June, with an implementation date for the new system set for a year later.

Strategic Considerations

The complexity of RYLC's IT ecosystem has affected its ability to grow through mergers and acquisitions, as integrating the business systems of other companies into the existing system landscape is very difficult. The board sees acquisitions as critical to RYLC's business strategy. The high-level focus group proposes three options for growth: merging with another car rental company that uses a more modern IT system to replace RYLC's IT infrastructure, offloading the complex IT systems to an outsourced company, or developing and implementing an entirely different strategy to modernize and simplify RYLC's application architecture.

Open questions that require attention include:

- Which technology would be best for implementing the system?
- Would building a new system internally be better than buying an off-the-shelf package?
- Which option would be most successful at integrating the package into a unified business-enabling infrastructure?

The high-level focus group believes that developing a new strategy to improve RYLC's application architecture will be beneficial. The board considers this to be a strategic challenge that requires RYLC to show continuous improvement over the next two years.

RYLC also identifies an opportunity to increase rental volume by collaborating with other companies in related but non-competing industries in order to create product bundles that have customer appeal. For instance, the company could collaborate with hotel chains to add rental cars or airport transportation to their accommodation packages. Such partnerships could introduce a new marketing channel to increase market share.

The board is also considering creating a virtual organization to collaborate with partner travel companies and group hotel, airline, and rental car reservations in all-in-one travel packages. This option offers lower setup costs and fewer risks than a merger and acquisition approach, and the planned SOA infrastructure will be capable of supporting such a virtual organization. The goal is to start looking for suitable business partners immediately, with the intention of conducting a working trial within six months.

Cloud Adoption

The company's IT systems run at near-maximum capacity early in the morning and in the late afternoon, when business customers are checking out or returning vehicles. Consumer demand also increases at seasonal peaks, especially around public and summer school holidays. Cloud-based IT resources can be used to efficiently manage system load and reduce overall computing costs by enabling additional capacity from a third-party cloud provider to be purchased on-demand, rather than investing in more on-site hardware.

The high-level focus group is considering making a deal with a commercial IT capacity trader or with foreign partners to share capacity. RYLC wants to concentrate on its core business of providing rental car services rather than expand its business focus to IT operations, and consequently launches efforts to look for suitable IT capacity traders right away.

The new CTO, Raj, is hired later that month. Raj has ten years of SOA and governance experience at a multinational investment bank and is a frequent convention speaker on SOA topics. RYLC's organizational restructuring takes place a week after Raj comes on board, in what would later be called the "Friday morning massacre."

All of the under-performing employees that had been reported to Robert are let go and provided with a competitive severance package and three months of outplacement assistance. While Robert lets go of most of the staff that worked in the departments that are now shut down, he keeps key employees who are perceived to be assets to the forming of a service-oriented enterprise. The most significant change is a realignment of all of the divisions and departments. The original structure of RYLC's divisions and departments is presented in Table 7.3.

The company's divisions and departments following the restructuring are presented in the heat map in Table 7.4.

Fleet management, sales, and marketing are no longer separate divisions but departments under the corporate division, which is now called the business development division. The IT division loses its data governance and application maintenance departments, the latter of which is now merged into systems development to reflect the dynamic nature of Robert's expectations for IT. Data governance will eventually become part of an enterprise-level governance office. Fleet management absorbs location management under the business development division. The profitability and market share department is removed due to the misleading nature of its name, and corporate acquisitions and product development become high-priority (highlighted in dark gray on the heat map).

Corporate	Fleet Management	Sales and Marketing	Information Technology
product development	vehicle purchasing	advertising and marketing campaigns	application maintenance
corporate acquisitions	vehicle maintenance	customer relations	systems development
profitability and market share	vehicle sales	vehicle delivery and collection	enterprise architecture
location management	vehicle cleaning	channel management	data governance
	vehicle availability	billing	

Table 7.3

Business Development	Information Technology
product development	systems development
corporate acquisitions	enterprise architecture
fleet management	
sales and marketing	

Table 7.4

Robert is not completely satisfied with this restructuring. The silos that existed between divisions and departments have now been eliminated, but more work needs to be done to truly succeed at establishing a next generation service-oriented enterprise. However, Wall Street responds favorably to RYLC's changes by adding six points to RYLC's stock price on heavy volume, despite lower than expected quarterly earnings and projections.

In August, Raj focuses on completing the vendor assessments before purchasing a vendor-based ESB SOA suite and an open-source tool set for testing, data access, change management, security management, and performance optimization. RYLC's ESB needs to enable integration and provide a virtualization layer for services orchestrated by the BPM engine. The new integration platform includes a number of key capabilities, most notably the ESB and BPM engine, that RYLC plans to leverage. The ESB contains all of the integration capabilities necessary to glue RYLC's systems together, while the BPM engine is intended for the automation of long-running and human-facing processes.

The integration between the car rental application and the CRM system is implemented using the integration solution as part of a proof of concept. The rental and sales processes are automated by the BPM engine, and integration between all of the automated processes and applications is achieved via Web service adapters. Different functions of the CRM system can be orchestrated and accessed directly using a legacy adapter provided by the integration engine.

The necessary transformation logic for the data mapping between different systems is embedded, which leads to tight coupling of business process logic to integration logic. As a result, the implemented process logic is almost impossible to reuse. RYLC's requirement for integration between systems and rapid delivery of functionality cannot be achieved in the current system, as underlying automation logic must be fundamentally changed for the integration or introduction of each new product.

To alleviate the service discoverability issue and lack of centralized documentation storage, Andrew recommends purchasing a registry/repository platform from the same vendor that supplied the company's ESB in order to leverage on the synergies and built-in integrations already existing between the two products.

Meanwhile, Raj hires an external consultant to lead a six-month project dedicated to transforming RYLC from a waterfall business model to an agile business model, as well as provide the company's developers and architects with on-site training in Web services, XML schema, and canonical data modeling. Headcount has continued to decline in the wake of the company's reorganization, and Raj has to spend time reassuring and motivating his team to provide the needed management. He also asks team members to confirm that the existing systems are still meeting service-level agreements.

New Reference Architecture

To stay competitive and make its operations more efficient, RYLC carefully reviews the current IT marketplace and selects the best technologies and solutions to meet its most critical needs. As RYLC begins its transformation journey by automating business processes and introducing SOA, its architects establish a reference architecture.

RYLC's conceptual architecture enables process automation and integration with back-end systems by establishing technology architecture via the application of select SOA design patterns. Many CRM features services are exposed via the ESB to avoid having to call CRM systems directly. Utility services providing workflow and rule processing logic are put in place with standardized service contracts. These steps help to achieve loose coupling between supporting systems, services, and underlying processes.

Services use different data models based on the systems with which they interact or expose. Since both domain and canonical data models had been implemented in different parts of the IT ecosystem, façade logic is added to facilitate translations between the models.

The newly introduced Notification service is an example of a utility-centric event service. Once a car rental is confirmed, the customer is notified through the preferred delivery method. The Notification service is invoked asynchronously as the last step in the process. The service interface is developed specifically to abstract the available event subscribers, delivery methods, and communication mechanisms. The ESB and the rule engine are used to route messages to the appropriate service consumers.

The Customer Profile Process

The company hires Ken, a lead service architect, who resolves the customer profile migration and integrity issues with a simple migration path leading away from the current group of inconsistent data silos. As part of Ken's grand solution, a new cloud-based Customer Profile service is developed to query, enter, and maintain customer profiles in a cloud environment. A new composite Customer Profile Migration service is created to assist in the gradual migration of customer information to a newly created cloud-based profile store, which is invoked whenever a customer profile search returns zero hits for a customer name. The service can invoke a series of utility services that act as wrappers for legacy systems to locate and retrieve data that matches the customer search criteria.

If no matching records are found, the Customer Profile Migration service invokes the cloud-based Customer Profile service, which allows the customer representative to record the details of the new customer. If a single matching record is found, the Customer Profile Migration service also invokes the Customer Profile service so that the representative can then check whether the profile is valid and up-to-date, make any necessary changes, and store the information as a new entry in the customer profile store. If multiple customer records are returned, the Customer Profile Migration service displays all of the record, thereby allowing the representative to select one. The chosen record results in the invocation of the Customer Profile service to provide the data for review or edits.

The process steps for the cloud-based Customer Profile service and Customer Profile Migration service are illustrated in Figure 7.1. The two services will ensure the accuracy and integrity of information in the customer profile store while only minimally impacting RYLC's existing clients. With the addition of the cloud-based service, each customer is asked to verify profile information only once after the first time they do business with RYLC.

Despite a number of technical issues with creating the wrapper logic for some of the legacy systems, the new Customer Profile and Vehicle Profile services become operational after four months. Preliminary surveys reveal a steady improvement in customer satisfaction and in the number of returning customers. The design team for the two services, which collectively represent the foundation for the development of RYLC's new Web site, is given the responsibility of managing RYLC's Internet sales channel. The IT division still needs to focus on strengthening CRM integration with the rental process, automating the fleet maintenance process, and developing a new sales process.

A task service is built to hide the details of how customer data is assembled from various sources, although RYLC plans to refine the architecture so that the integration logic for the concrete CRM systems can be moved to entity services. Once this is achieved, the task service can compose the entity service calls to the underlying CRM systems. This solution proves to be effective months down the road, when one of the CRM systems has to be phased out without changing the interfaces that are exposed through task and entity services. As a result, none of the consuming systems require modification.

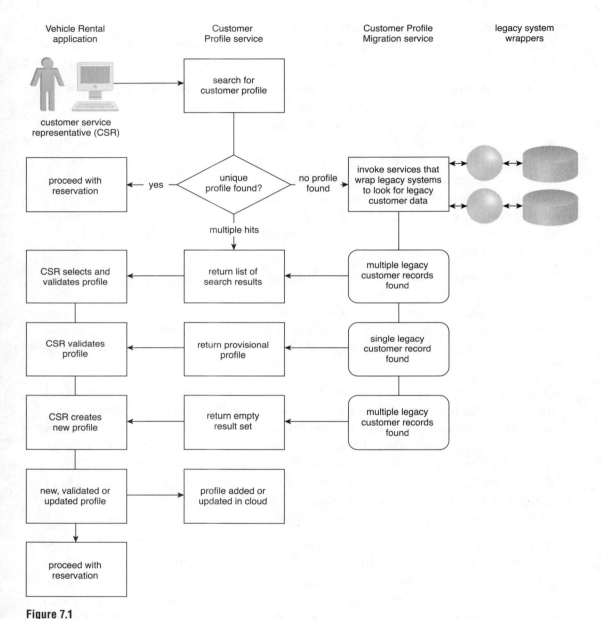

Figure 7.1

A flowchart outlining the steps for the customer profile business process, as carried out by the Customer Profile and Customer Profile Migration services.

Raj briefs Jesse and Robert on RYLC's progress and architectural reference plan in September. Raj then asks his business analyst team to model the company's car rental process using BPM and BPMN. The team has many discussions about whether modeling the complete process end-to-end is better than breaking it along longer logical boundaries. An advantage of an overarching, end-to-end process is that all of the critical steps can be displayed in a single model, although the process structure will most likely change over time because certain steps are more prone to change than others. After multiple rounds of talks, RYLC's architects and business analysts finally decide that isolating each sub-process offers more benefits than maintaining the entire process as a whole.

New Service Technology

Management in the business development division want definitive answers as to how new proposed service technologies will help RYLC's bottom line. Mary insists that the IT team has to update the reference architecture to include hard metrics, milestones, and ROI measures. She believes that the additional funding that is being devoted to SOA could be better used for marketing. Raj pitches several business facilitators that she meets with skepticism. After lengthy talks, she finally agrees to an SOA plan with the following characteristics:

- *Business Intelligence* – To obtain realtime information on sales, purchasing, and customer behavior, newly engineered processes will be instrumented with business activity monitors that display aggregated information on the status of RYLC's entire fleet of rental cars, as well as current trends for business users.

- *Complex Event Processing* – To help identify trends and aggregate in-house transactional data with external market events, data can be fed into the global data warehouse system to evaluate and analyze trends over time.

- *Event-Driven Architecture* – COBOL-based legacy CRM systems can be SOA-enabled through the use of events. An XML-based event structure can be created for each business transaction, and each event based on this structure can then be posted to an accessible queuing system.

Within the company's enterprise portal, users are provided with a feature that enables them to store their own "places of interest." This functionality is currently achieved by invoking the back-end COBOL APIs, which create and issue events. In contrast, an

SOA-enabled BPM process can be registered to listen to the profile. After receiving the event, the SOA process engine executes a new BPMN process called "Advertisements for New Holidays."

EDA can also enable realtime decision-making, which can help to resolve inventory discrepancies due to vehicles being returned by customers to a different location than the one that rented out the vehicle. To reconcile RYLC's inventory with customer deliveries, the car check-in and check-out services can generate a type of event that would send check-in and check-out information. The CEP engine can pick up the produced events and create new business events that are dependent on the aforementioned business rule and additional event streams, such as a customer traveling close to the location. To further reconcile inventory delivery imbalances, another rule is defined to generate special promotions the apply whenever a customer returns over 50% of its rented vehicles to the original location.

Raj is particularly enthusiastic about the prospect of using information provided by service execution and business event monitoring to present realtime views. His goal is to provide executives and senior managers with a portal that displays a dashboard capable of showing the current state of the business activities, comparison of historical trends, and highlighting of potential issues as soon as they become apparent. The business development division believes the dashboard has the potential to make a major contribution to customer satisfaction.

Next, Robert asks Raj to identify a business case for a Big Data initiative and further establish a strategy for its implementation if the business case proves to be valuable. Raj and his data architect meet with various divisions within RYLC as well as a number of IT teams, and determine two use cases that offer the best value for the organization. The first focus is on the collection and analysis of customer feedback from a variety of social and travel Web sites. The second use case is the realtime analysis of application logs to identify problems and alert relevant support teams. Robert agrees to begin work on these use cases and provides initial funding to implement a proof of concept and establish a preliminary infrastructure footprint.

For the first use case, a cloud-based Hadoop tool is implemented for customer feedback analysis. A number of Web sites where customers have left feedback about their experience with RYLC are identified, and feeds are built to capture the information. Hadoop is used to analyze all the collected information and identify key trends. Services are built to expose the results to RYLC's existing BI tools so that they can be published in a daily report for the CEO and his team.

For the second use case, the development team decides to use a vendor tool to carry out realtime analysis because log files currently cannot be moved to a cloud provider quickly or easily enough to enable realtime processing. The tool is configured to look for specific problems and events across all application logs. If a situation is identified where a specific action is required, the existing alert service is invoked to notify the appropriate teams of the discovered anomaly. Even though the proof of concept is limited to a small sample size and to a subset of the expected problem space, it is so successful that Jesse tasks Robert with expediting the full roll-out schedule and identifying additional use cases where Big Data can be beneficial.

As a final stage to RYLC's initial service technology adoption project, RYLC establishes a mobile communication strategy. The first part of this initiative is to empower customers to rent a car via classic Web interfaces and mobile devices. Successful implementation would allow customers to use a mobile device to order a rental car with premium features, such as delivery to a specific location within 30 minutes. Alternatively, customers can use instant checkout at self-serve terminals instead of waiting to complete the details with a sales agent at the counter. The second component of RYLC's strategy is related to paperless damage report management. Agents can use mobile devices, such as tablets, to record rental car damage in a report that is routed electronically to the service station. The final component of the strategy relates to a business model called reverse logistics, by which a collection of cars can be outsourced from different locations, and routing information for the collecting agency can be provided through mobile devices.

The SOA Governance Program Office

To establish the appropriate foundation for RYLC's transformation, Robert and Raj decide to implement a BPM engine to automate new business processes so that they are no longer hardwired into the applications. Concurrent agile sprints are launched in August and RYLC finishes building its first service by mid-September, with additional services scheduled to go online every two weeks thereafter.

In October, RYLC establishes a central SOA Governance Program Office (SGPO) to resolve enterprise-wide conflict and disputes, which have been especially pronounced between the IT and business development divisions. Agile teams have begun to build and move services into production without any executive oversight or informing other teams. Developers are frustrated with the lack of direction regarding project funding, while multiple projects declare that they are being unfairly burdened with paying for a service that other teams were also using. Meanwhile, project managers are unsure about which methodology to apply for service delivery, what deliverables are necessary, and how existing services should be introduced and implemented.

The SGPO is chartered with establishing all SOA governance precepts and processes, setting up a standard funding model, and continually revitalizing the program. Andrew proposes combining the SGPO with the IT division and is faced with opposition from Mary, who states that governance needs to reflect RYLC's business interests and not its technology interests. Robert agrees with Mary and declares that the business development division will own the SGPO, which is to be chaired by Andrew alongside representatives from each IT department and enterprise architects from other domains, such as data, security, infrastructure, and common assets. The SGPO will have a dotted relationship to RYLC's board itself in order to provide technical advice to the steering committee. The steering committee is expanded to include the CIO, chief architect, and all business division heads, and has been specifically mandated to work closely with the SGPO in aligning business strategies with SOA and measuring results.

The SGPO decides to establish a central platform funding approach and recommends adopting a hybrid funding model for service delivery work. The central funding model releases money from the enterprise rather than from project budgets, whereas a hybrid funding model is a combination of both project funding and central funding approaches.

The SGPO also establishes the SOA project lifecycle by defining a comprehensive set of precepts and processes, along with the corresponding roles for each stage in the lifecycle. A set of operational metrics with which to measure the performance of each precept and process is also identified.

The Enterprise Architecture Board

The problems surrounding the new integration platform reveal to RYLC's upper management that the solution is too strongly influenced by IT and silo-based considerations. In response, Raj advises that the company set up an enterprise architecture board with an emphasis on SOA/BPM. Raj argues that the board can be empowered to design and govern solutions with a broad, enterprise-wide perspective focused on important business processes and information spread across multiple applications and departments. Setting up the enterprise architecture board allows the company to move towards separating process and integration logic by establishing SOA and BPM strategies and governance controls, creating a comprehensive system roadmap, and prioritizing IT investments.

The board outlines the three following steps as a means of achieving RYLC's business objectives:

- Strengthen CRM integration in the rental process to achieve better data quality for increased customer satisfaction. To achieve this, the rental application needs to be expanded and the rental process provided with access to services from the CRM. The implementation will then be able to eliminate the batch interface with the CRM and improve the quality and concurrency of data.

- Automate the fleet maintenance process to minimize breakdowns and increase customer satisfaction. A customer's return of a vehicle can trigger a service check that removes the car from the rental process. Services need to be further developed so that they can communicate with the vehicle rental application that manages car purchases, repairs, and sales.

- Develop a new sales process that allows customers to book rental cars online, via a Web browser or a mobile platform. The rental application needs to provide either the rental process or its sub-processes with a service for customers to access online. Additional user and rights management capabilities are required in order to allow customers to access the sales process directly. Additionally, a new channel-specific user-interface that is interoperable for acquisitions can be developed for both internal employees and customers to use.

RYLC's updated organizational structure as of October is summarized in Table 7.5.

Business Development	Information Technology
product development	systems development
corporate acquisitions	enterprise architecture
fleet management	
sales and marketing	
governance	

Table 7.5
The updated RYLC organizational structure in October.

A Transformed Enterprise

By the third week of October, RYLC has an operating governance department that transmits service-centric metrics throughout the enterprise, with a growing inventory of services and a stable headcount.

Fimalac SA's Fitch Ratings raises RYLC's credit rating from C to A+, citing "adequate containment on risk governance issues" without any reference to its service-orientation initiatives. The hedge fund that has representation on RYLC's board increases its holdings by five percent. Wall Street announces that RYLC stock is a buy with strong ratios, earnings, and discounted cash flows. Technical analysts observe the bullish Golden Swan pattern in a five-year breakout into virgin territory on heavy volume in the middle of November, with the company's stock valuation having increased by 113 million dollars since the middle of April. Halfway into December, Robert prompts his IT management team for a review of the SOA rollout progress.

RYLC has experienced great change over the past six months. High-priority issues relating to customer relations and vehicle maintenance have been addressed. The company has survived an enterprise-wide reorganization. An ESB has been purchased, a service inventory, reference architecture, and canonical data model have been created, and SOA governance has been established. Although the initiative to offshore customer service to Malaysia missed the December deadline, the transition is still tracking, as is the Texas acquisition.

Two franchise agreements in southeast Asia have opened up a new revenue stream. Robert wants to fuel this momentum by expanding into Vietnam, India, and the People's Republic of China. In January, Mary and her team plan a trip to Ireland, Great Britain, Sweden, and France to explore business opportunities and develop partnerships. The board and senior management are convinced that both their business model and IT resources can be effectively scaled.

Robert presents the before and after snapshots of RYLC's progress using the revised heat maps, as shown in Tables 7.6 and 7.7.

Corporate	Fleet Management	Sales and Marketing	Information Technology
product development	vehicle purchasing	advertising and marketing campaigns	application maintenance
corporate acquisitions	vehicle maintenance	customer relations	systems development
profitability and market share	vehicle sales	vehicle delivery and collection	enterprise architecture
location management	cleaning	channel management	data governance
	vehicle availability	billing	

Table 7.6
Before: The RYLC organizational structure in March.

Business Development	Information Technology
product development	systems development
corporate acquisitions	enterprise architecture
fleet management	
sales and marketing	
governance	

Table 7.7
After: The RYLC organizational structure in December.

Trust between the SPGO and the enterprise has developed. The employees are embracing working from home with alacrity, as this arrangement enables them to participate more effectively across multiple time zones while minimizing impact on their personal lives. Human resources leverages this work structure as an incentive for attracting more high-caliber talent. However, some directors and managers find that they require on-site presence to better facilitate communication and execution. Robert is renegotiating the lease on RYLC's headquarters in anticipation of downsizing to a building that is more suitable for the new employee work model. Cloud-based delivery of configuration, storage, and bandwidth is moving along. Jane and other board members are pleased to see that the cloud usage metrics are trending in the right direction. RYLC's inventory of high-value services is growing and in use throughout the enterprise.

More importantly, shareholders and customers alike are starting to take notice of the company's transformation, resulting in rising stock prices and growing market share. The marketing department starts producing brand-specific television commercials and rolls out a new social media initiative to highlight company successes. They are also planning a presentation for an upcoming industry trade show.

Despite the many positive developments, the company is still facing data quality issues associated with heterogeneous databases, a lack of deployment automation, and employee resistance to agile, as well as superficial reporting from organically developed fact tables from the business intelligence team. To address these issues, Robert develops an agenda to identify a homogeneous tool set and develop deployment automation. He also launches an effort to create an enterprise information integration layer to provide common data and metadata, before replacing the business intelligence manager.

Now looking ahead to the first quarter of the following year, RYLC's senior management focuses on celebrating the company's achievements of the past nine months. As a result of Mary's foray into European markets, the board now has the confidence to add ten cents to their dividend, increase the price of half of RYLC's service offerings to bolster profit margins, and cut prices in certain markets to undermine competition. The board challenges Robert to continue building relations with cruise lines, hotels, and resorts based in the United States, with the intention of branching out with international partners in the next five years.

Robert approves the redesign of the company's Web site to include a travel forum that can attract more traffic and reduce showrooming (clicking from RYLC's Web site to rival sites for price comparison). In February, he also proposes launching the RYLC University as a one-week boot camp for all employees, from the CEO to the most recent hire, to raise awareness of RYLC's service-oriented culture and values and to further provide practical customer service guidance.

These initiatives result in an escalating demand for new services and composite solutions. RYLC's analysts and developers rise to the challenge by further enriching the company's service portfolio with high-value services. Major competitors throughout the industry are beginning to branch out beyond the typical SOA implementation. In response, RYLC dedicates efforts to adopting and extending emerging service technologies in its transition to better reposition services for accommodating business and organizational changes.

From recent surveys of its customers, RYLC can see marked improvements in the responsiveness and quality of the delivery of its services. The company will continue to seek out opportunities for acquisitions and ways to leverage new technologies.

Appendices

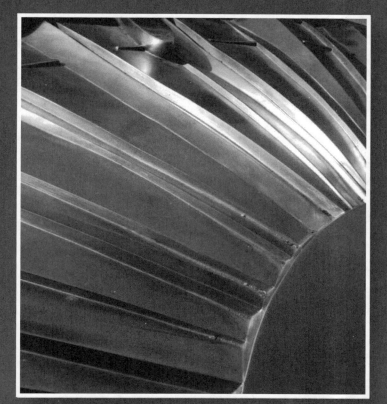

Additional Reading for Applying Service-Orientation

The Eight Service-Orientation Principles

The Four Characteristics of SOA

SOA Design Patterns

This appendix provides supplementary reading reasources for the topics covered in the *Applying Service-Orientation* section from Chapter 2. The content in this appendix is comprised of condensed excerpts from the *SOA Principles of Service Design* and *SOA Design Patterns* series titles.

The Eight Service-Orientation Principles

This section provides profile tables for the eight design principles that are documented in *SOA Principles of Service Design*, a title that is part of this book series.

Every profile table contains the following sections:

- *Short Definition* – A concise, single-statement definition that establishes the fundamental purpose of the principle.

- *Long Definition* – A longer description of the principle that provides more detail as to what it is intended to accomplish.

- *Goals* – A list of specific design goals that are expected from the application of the principle. Essentially, this list provides the ultimate results of the principle's realization.

- *Design Characteristics* – A list of specific design characteristics that can be realized via the application of the principle. This provides some insight as to how the principle ends up shaping the service.

- *Implementation Requirements* – A list of common prerequisites for effectively applying the design principle. These can range from technology to organizational requirements.

Note that these tables provide only summarized content from the original publication. Information about service-orientation principles is also published online at www.soaprinciples.com and www.serviceorientation.com.

Standardized Service Contract	
Short Definition	*"Services share standardized contracts."*
Long Definition	*"Services within the same service inventory are in compliance with the same contract design standards."*
Goals	• To enable services with a meaningful level of natural interoperability within the boundary of a service inventory. This reduces the need for data transformation because consistent data models are used for information exchange. • To allow the purpose and capabilities of services to be more easily and intuitively understood. The consistency with which service functionality is expressed through service contracts increases interpretability and the overall predictability of service endpoints throughout a service inventory. Note that these goals are further supported by other service-orientation principles as well.
Design Characteristics	• A service contract (comprised of a technical interface or one or more service description documents) is provided with the service. • The service contract is standardized through the application of design standards.
Implementation Requirements	The fact that contracts need to be standardized can introduce significant implementation requirements to organizations that do not have a history of using standards. For example: • Design standards and conventions need to ideally be in place prior to the delivery of any service in order to ensure adequately scoped standardization. (For those organizations that have already produced ad-hoc Web services, retro-fitting strategies may need to be employed.) • Formal processes need to be introduced to ensure that services are modeled and designed consistently, incorporating accepted design principles, conventions, and standards.

- Because achieving standardized service contracts generally requires a "contract-first" approach to service-oriented design, the full application of this principle will often demand the use of development tools capable of importing a customized service contract without imposing changes.

- Appropriate skill sets are required to carry out the modeling and design processes with the chosen tools. When working with Web services, the need for a high level of proficiency with XML schema and WSDL languages is practically unavoidable. WS-Policy expertise may also be required.

These and other requirements can add up to a noticeable transition effort that goes well beyond technology adoption.

Table A.1
A profile for the Standardized Service Contract principle

Service Loose Coupling	
Short Definition	*"Services are loosely coupled."*
Long Definition	*"Service contracts impose low consumer coupling requirements and are themselves decoupled from their surrounding environment."*
Goals	By consistently fostering reduced coupling within and between services we are working toward a state where service contracts increase independence from their implementations and services are increasingly independent from each other. This promotes an environment in which services and their consumers can be adaptively evolved over time with minimal impact on each other.
Design Characteristics	• The existence of a service contract that is ideally decoupled from technology and implementation details. • A functional service context that is not dependent on outside logic. • Minimal consumer coupling requirements.
Implementation Requirements	• Loosely coupled services are typically required to perform more runtime processing than if they were more tightly coupled. As a result, data exchange in general can consume more runtime resources, especially during concurrent access and high usage scenarios. • Achieving the right balance of coupling, while also supporting the other service-orientation principles that affect contract design, requires increased service contract design proficiency.

Table A.2

A profile for the Service Loose Coupling principle

Service Abstraction	
Short Definition	*"Non-essential service information is abstracted."*
Long Definition	*"Service contracts only contain essential information and information about services is limited to what is published in service contracts."*
Goals	Many of the other principles emphasize the need to publish *more* information in the service contract. The primary role of this principle is to keep the quantity and detail of contract content concise and balanced and prevent unnecessary access to additional service details.
Design Characteristics	• Services consistently abstract specific information about technology, logic, and function away from the outside world (the world outside of the service boundary). • Services have contracts that concisely define interaction requirements and constraints and other required service meta details. • Outside of what is documented in the service contract, information about a service is controlled or altogether hidden within a particular environment.
Implementation Requirements	The primary prerequisite to achieving the appropriate level of abstraction for each service is the level of service contract design skill applied.

Table A.3

A profile for the Service Abstraction principle

Service Reusability	
Short Definition	*"Services are reusable."*
Long Definition	*"Services contain and express agnostic logic and can be positioned as reusable enterprise resources."*
Goals	The goals behind Service Reusability are tied directly to some of the most strategic objectives of service-oriented computing: • To allow for service logic to be repeatedly leveraged over time so as to achieve an increasingly high return on the initial investment of delivering the service. • To increase business agility on an organizational level by enabling the rapid fulfillment of future business automation requirements through wide-scale service composition. • To enable the realization of agnostic service models. • To enable the creation of service inventories with a high percentage of agnostic services.
Design Characteristics	• The logic encapsulated by the service is associated with a context that is sufficiently agnostic to any one usage scenario so as to be considered reusable. • The logic encapsulated by the service is sufficiently generic, allowing it to facilitate numerous usage scenarios by different types of service consumers. • The service contract is flexible enough to process a range of input and output messages. • Services are designed to facilitate simultaneous access by multiple consumer programs.

Implementation Requirements	From an implementation perspective, Service Reusability can be the most demanding of the principles we've covered so far. Below are common requirements for creating reusable services and supporting their long-term existence: • A scalable runtime hosting environment capable of high-to-extreme concurrent service usage. Once a service inventory is relatively mature, reusable services will find themselves in an increasingly large number of compositions. • A solid version control system to properly evolve contracts representing reusable services. • Service analysts and designers with a high degree of subject matter expertise who can ensure that the service boundary and contract accurately represent the service's reusable functional context. • A high level of service development and commercial software development expertise so as to structure the underlying logic into generic and potentially decomposable components and routines. These and other requirements place an emphasis on the appropriate staffing of the service delivery team, as well as the importance of a powerful and scalable hosting environment and supporting infrastructure.

Table A.4

A profile for the Service Reusability principle

Service Autonomy	
Short Definition	*"Services are autonomous."*
Long Definition	*"Services exercise a high level of control over their underlying runtime execution environment."*
Goals	• To increase a service's runtime reliability, performance, and predictability, especially when being reused and composed. • To increase the amount of control a service has over its runtime environment. By pursuing autonomous design and runtime environments, we are essentially aiming to increase post-implementation control over the service and the service's control over its own execution environment.
Design Characteristics	• Services have a contract that expresses a well-defined functional boundary that should not overlap with other services. • Services are deployed in an environment over which they exercise a great deal (and preferably an exclusive level) of control. • Service instances are hosted by an environment that accommodates high concurrency for scalability purposes.
Implementation Requirements	• A high level of control over how service logic is designed and developed. Depending on the level of autonomy being sought, this may also involve control over the supporting data models. • A distributable deployment environment, so as to allow the service to be moved, isolated, or composed as required. • An infrastructure capable of supporting desired autonomy levels.

Table A.5

A profile for the Service Autonomy principle

Service Statelessness	
Short Definition	*"Services minimize statefulness."*
Long Definition	*"Services minimize resource consumption by deferring the management of state information when necessary."*
Goals	• To increase service scalability. • To support the design of agnostic service logic and improve the potential for service reuse.
Design Characteristics	What makes this somewhat of a unique principle is the fact that it is promoting a condition of the service that is temporary in nature. Depending on the service model and state deferral approach used, different types of design characteristics can be implemented. Some examples include: • Highly business process-agnostic logic so that the service is not designed to retain state information for any specific parent business process. • Less constrained service contracts so as to allow for the receipt and transmission of a wider range of state data at runtime. • Increased amounts of interpretive programming routines capable of parsing a range of state information delivered by messages and responding to a range of corresponding action requests.
Implementation Requirements	Although state deferral can reduce the overall consumption of memory and system resources, services designed with state-lessness considerations can also introduce some performance demands associated with the runtime retrieval and interpretation of deferred state data. Here is a short checklist of common requirements that can be used to assess the support of stateless service designs by vendor technologies and target deployment locations: • The runtime environment should allow for a service to transition from an idle state to an active processing state in a highly efficient manner.

- Enterprise-level or high-performance XML parsers and hardware accelerators (and SOAP processors) should be provided to allow services implemented as Web services to more efficiently parse larger message payloads with less performance constraints.

- The use of attachments may need to be supported by Web services to allow messages to include bodies of payload data that do not undergo interface-level validation or translation to local formats.

The nature of the implementation support required by the average stateless service in an environment will depend on the state deferral approach used within the service-oriented architecture.

Table A.6
A profile for the Service Statelessness principle

Service Discoverability	
Short Definition	*"Services are discoverable."*
Long Definition	*"Services are supplemented with communicative metadata by which they can be effectively discovered and interpreted."*
Goals	• Services are positioned as highly discoverable resources within the enterprise. • The purpose and capabilities of each service are clearly expressed so that they can be interpreted by humans and software programs. Achieving these goals requires foresight and a solid understanding of the nature of the service itself. Depending on the type of service model being designed, realizing this principle may require both business and technical expertise.
Design Characteristics	• Service contracts are equipped with appropriate metadata that will be correctly referenced when discovery queries are issued. • Service contracts are further outfitted with additional meta information that clearly communicates their purpose and capabilities to humans. • If a service registry exists, registry records are populated with the same attention to meta information as just described. • If a service registry does not exist, service profile documents are authored to supplement the service contract and to form the basis for future registry records.

Implementation Requirements	• The existence of design standards that govern the meta information used to make service contracts discoverable and interpretable, as well as guidelines for how and when service contracts should be further supplemented with annotations.
	• The existence of design standards that establish a consistent means of recording service meta information outside of the contract. This information is either collected in a supplemental document in preparation for a service registry, or is placed in the registry itself.
	You may have noticed the absence of a service registry on the list of implementation requirements. As previously established, the goal of this principle is to implement design characteristics within the service, not within the architecture.

Table A.7

A profile for the Service Discoverability principle

Service Composability	
Short Definition	*"Services are composable."*
Long Definition	*"Services are effective composition participants, regardless of the size and complexity of the composition."*
Goals	When discussing the goals of Service Composability, most of the goals of Service Reusability apply. This is because service composition often turns out to be a form of service reuse. In fact, you may recall that one of the objectives we listed for the Service Reusability principle was to enable wide-scale service composition. However, above and beyond simply attaining reuse, service composition provides the medium through which we can achieve what is often classified as the ultimate goal of service-oriented computing. By establishing an enterprise comprised of solution logic represented by an inventory of highly reusable services, we provide the means for a large extent of future business automation requirements to be fulfilled through service composition.
Design Characteristics For Composition Member Capabilities	Ideally, every service capability (especially those providing reusable logic) is considered a potential composition member. This essentially means that the design characteristics already established by the Service Reusability principle are equally relevant to building effective composition members. Additionally, there are two further characteristics emphasized by this principle: • The service needs to possess a highly efficient execution environment. More so than being able to manage concurrency, the efficiency with which composition members perform their individual processing should be highly tuned. • The service contract needs to be flexible so that it can facilitate different types of data exchange requirements for similar functions. This typically relates to the ability of the contract to exchange the same type of data at different levels of granularity. The manner in which these qualities go beyond mere reuse has to do primarily with the service being capable of optimizing its runtime processing responsibilities in support of multiple, simultaneous compositions.

Design Characteristics for Composition Controller Capabilities	Composition members will often also need to act as controllers or sub-controllers within different composition configurations. However, services designed as designated controllers are generally alleviated from many of the high-performance demands placed on composition members. These types of services therefore have their own set of design characteristics: • The logic encapsulated by a designated controller will almost always be limited to a single business task. Typically, the task service model is used, resulting in the common characteristics of that model being applied to this type of service. • While designated controllers may be reusable, service reuse is not usually a primary design consideration. Therefore, the design characteristics fostered by Service Reusability are considered and applied where appropriate, but with less of the usual rigor applied to agnostic services. • Statelessness is not always as strictly emphasized on designated controllers as with composition members. Depending on the state deferral options available by the surrounding architecture, designated controllers may sometimes need to be designed to remain fully stateful while the underlying composition members carry out their respective parts of the overall task. Of course, any capability acting as a controller can become a member of a larger composition, which brings the previously listed composition member design characteristics into account as well.

Table A.8

A profile for the Service Composability principle

The Four Characteristics of SOA

Having just explained the service-orientation design paradigm and its associated goals, we now need to turn our attention to the physical design of a service-oriented solution or environment.

In support of achieving the goals of service-orientation, there are four base characteristics we look to establish in any form of SOA:

- Business-Driven
- Vendor-Independent
- Enterprise-Centric
- Composition-Centric

These characteristics help distinguish SOA from other architectural models and also define the fundamental requirements a technology architecture must fulfill to be fully supportive of service-orientation. As we explore each individually, keep in mind that in real-world implementations the extent to which these characteristics can be attained will likely vary.

Business-Driven

Traditional technology architectures were commonly designed in support of solutions delivered to fulfill tactical (short-term) business requirements. Because the overarching, strategic (long-term) business goals of the organization aren't taken into consideration when the architecture is defined, this approach can result in a technical environment that, over time, falls out of alignment with the organization's business direction and requirements.

This gradual separation of business and technology results in a technology architecture with diminishing potential to fulfill business requirements and one that is increasingly difficult to adapt to changing business needs (Figure A.1).

When a technology architecture is business-driven, the overarching business vision, goals, and requirements are positioned as the basis for and the primary influence of the architectural model. This maximizes the potential alignment of technology and business and allows for a technology architecture that can evolve in tandem with the organization as a whole (Figure A.2). The result is a continual increase in the value and lifespan of the architecture.

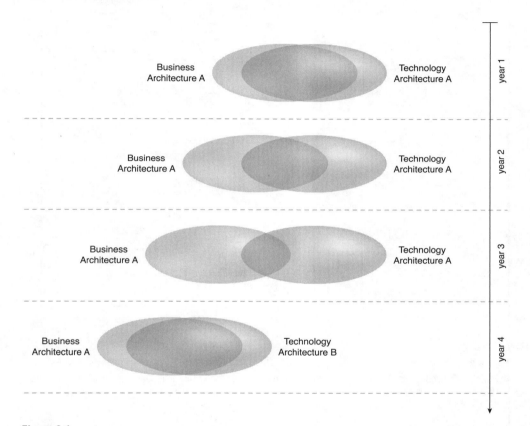

Figure A.1

A traditional technology architecture (A) is often delivered in alignment with the current state of a business but can be incapable of changing in alignment with how the business evolves. As business and technology architectures become increasingly out of sync, business requirement fulfillment decreases, often to the point that a whole new technology architecture (B) is needed, which effectively resets this cycle.

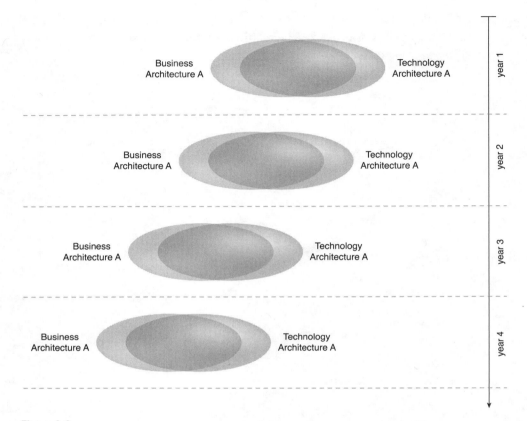

Figure A.2

By defining a strategic, business-centric scope to the technology architecture, it can be kept in constant sync with how the business evolves over time.

Vendor-Neutral

Designing a service-oriented technology architecture around one particular vendor platform can lead to an implementation that inadvertently inherits proprietary characteristics. This can end up inhibiting the future evolution of an inventory architecture in response to technology innovations that become available from other vendors.

An inhibitive technology architecture is unable to evolve and expand in response to changing automation requirements, which can result in the architecture having a limited lifespan after which it needs to be replaced to remain effective (Figure A.3).

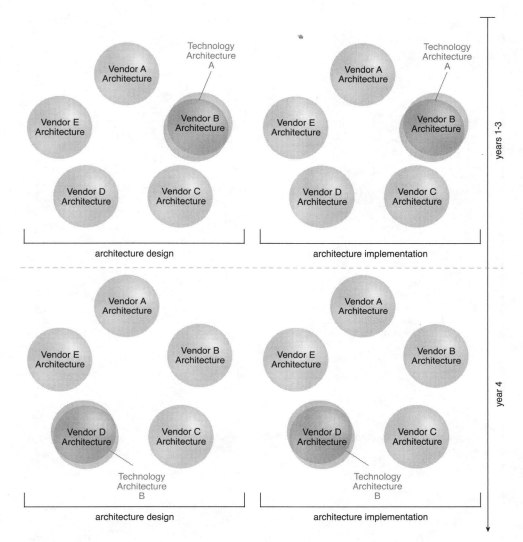

Figure A.3
Vendor-centric technology architectures are often bound to corresponding vendor platform roadmaps. This can reduce opportunities to leverage technology innovations provided by other vendor platforms and can result in the need to eventually replace the architecture entirely with a new vendor implementation (which starts the cycle over again).

It is in the best interest of an organization to base the design of a service-oriented architecture on a model that is in alignment with the primary SOA vendor platforms, yet neutral to all of them (Figuer A.4). A vendor-neutral architectural model can be derived from a vendor-neutral design paradigm used to build the solution logic the architecture will be responsible for supporting. The service-orientation paradigm provides such an approach, in that it is derived from and applicable to real-world technology platforms while remaining neutral to them.

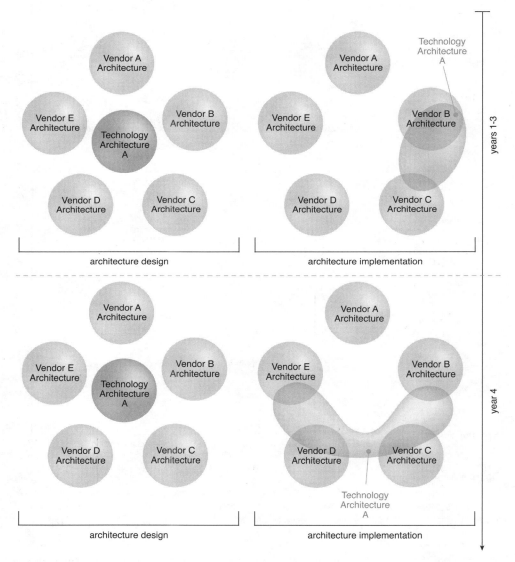

Figure A.4
If the architectural model is designed to be and remain neutral to vendor platforms, it maintains the freedom to diversify its implementation by leveraging multiple vendor technology innovations. This increases the longevity of the architecture as it is allowed to augment and evolve in response to changing requirements.

Enterprise-Centric

The fact that service-oriented solutions are based on a distributed architecture doesn't mean that there still isn't the constant danger of creating new silos within an enterprise when building poorly designed services, as illustrated in Figure A.5.

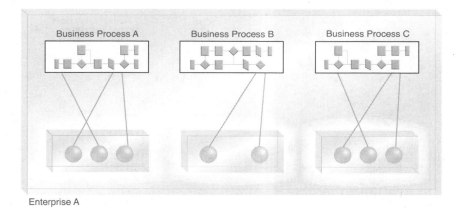

Figure A.5

Single-purpose services delivered to automate specific business processes can end up establishing silos within the enterprise.

When applying service-orientation, services are positioned as *enterprise resources*, which implies that service logic is designed with the following primary characteristics:

* The logic is available beyond a specific implementation boundary.

* The logic is designed according to established design principles and enterprise standards.

Essentially, the body of logic is classified as a resource of the enterprise. This does not necessarily make it an enterprise-*wide* resource or one that must be used throughout an entire technical environment. An enterprise resource is simply logic positioned as an IT asset; an extension of the enterprise that does not belong solely to any one application or solution. As further established in the pattern description for Service Encapsulation, an enterprise resource essentially embodies the fundamental characteristics of service logic.

In order to leverage services as enterprise resources, the underlying technology architecture must establish a model that is natively based on the assumption that software programs delivered as services will be shared by other parts of the enterprise or will be part of larger solutions that include shared services. This baseline requirement places an emphasis on standardizing parts of the architecture so that service reuse and interoperability can be continually fostered (Figure A.6).

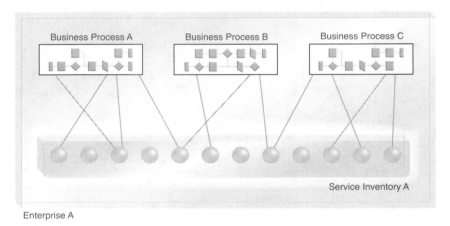

Figure A.6

When services are positioned as enterprise resources, they no longer create or reside in silos. Instead they are made available to a broader scope of utilization by being part of a service inventory.

Composition-Centric

More so than in previous distributed computing paradigms, service-orientation places an emphasis on designing software programs as not just reusable resources, but as flexible resources that can be plugged into different aggregate structures for a variety of service-oriented solutions.

To accomplish this, services must be composable. As advocated by the Service Composability principle, this means that services must be capable of being pulled into a variety of composition designs, regardless of whether or not they are initially required to participate in a composition when they are first delivered (A.7).

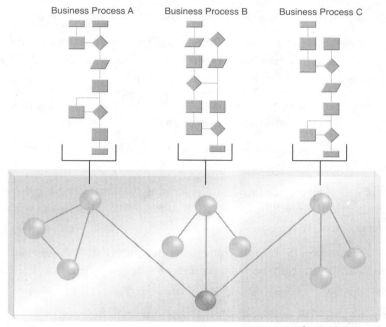

Figure A.7
Services within the same service inventory are composed into different configurations.
The highlighted service is reused by multiple compositions to automate different
business processes.

To support native composability, the underlying technology architecture must be prepared to enable a range of simple and complex composition designs. Architectural extensions (and related infrastructure extensions) pertaining to scalability, reliability, and runtime data exchange processing and integrity are essential to support this key characteristic.

SOA Design Patterns

This section provides profile tables for the seven patterns that correspond to the seven steps covered in Chapter 3, as well as the two service inventory patterns referenced in different parts of the book. Every profile table contains the following sections:

- *Requirement* – A requirement is a concise, single-sentence statement that presents the fundamental requirement addressed by the pattern in the form of a question. Every pattern description begins with this statement.

- *Problem* – The issue causing a problem and the effects of the problem. It is this problem for which the pattern is expected to provide a solution.

- *Solution* – This represents the design solution proposed by the pattern to solve the problem and fulfill the requirement.

- *Application* – This part is dedicated to describing how the pattern can be applied. It can include guidelines, implementation details, and sometimes even a suggested process.

- *Impacts* – This section highlights common consequences, costs, and requirements associated with the application of a pattern and may also provide alternatives that can be considered.

- *Principles* – References to related service-orientation principles.

- *Architecture* – References to related SOA architecture types.

Note that these tables provide only summarized content from the original publication. Detailed pattern descriptions with examples are provided in the *SOA Design Patterns* series title. Summarized profile tables of the entire SOA design patterns catalog are also published online at www.soapatterns.org.

Agnostic Capability

By Thomas Erl

How can multi-purpose service logic be made effectively consumable and composable?

Problem	Service capabilities derived from specific concerns may not be useful to multiple service consumers, thereby reducing the reusability potential of the agnostic service.
Solution	Agnostic service logic is partitioned into a set of well-defined capabilities that address common concerns not specific to any one problem. Through subsequent analysis, the agnostic context of capabilities is further refined.
Application	Service capabilities are defined and iteratively refined through proven analysis and modeling processes.
Impacts	The definition of each service capability requires extra up-front analysis and design effort.
Principles	Standardized Service Contract, Service Reusability, Service Composability
Architecture	Service

Agnostic Context

By Thomas Erl

How can multi-purpose service logic be positioned as an effective enterprise resource?

Problem	Multi-purpose logic grouped together with single-purpose logic results in programs with little or no reuse potential that introduce waste and redundancy into an enterprise.
Solution	Isolate logic that is not specific to one purpose into separate services with distinct agnostic contexts.
Application	Agnostic service contexts are defined by carrying out service-oriented analysis and service modeling processes.
Impacts	This pattern positions reusable solution logic at an enterprise level, potentially bringing with it increased design complexity and enterprise governance issues.
Principles	Service Reusability
Architecture	Service

Capability Composition
By Thomas Erl

How can a service capability solve a problem that requires logic outside of the service boundary?

Problem	A capability may not be able to fulfill its processing requirements without adding logic that resides outside of its service's functional context, thereby compromising the integrity of the service context and risking service denormalization.
Solution	When requiring access to logic that falls outside of a service's boundary, capability logic within the service is designed to compose one or more capabilities in other services.
Application	The functionality encapsulated by a capability includes logic that can invoke other capabilities from other services.
Impacts	Carrying out composition logic requires external invocation, which adds performance overhead and decreases service autonomy.
Principles	All
Architecture	Inventory, Composition, Service

Capability Recomposition

By Thomas Erl

How can the same capability be used to help solve multiple problems?

Problem	Using agnostic service logic to only solve a single problem is wasteful and does not leverage the logic's reuse potential.
Solution	Agnostic service capabilities can be designed to be repeatedly invoked in support of multiple compositions that solve multiple problems.
Application	Effective recomposition requires the coordinated, successful, and repeated application of several additional patterns.
Impacts	Repeated service composition demands existing and persistent standardization and governance.
Principles	All
Architecture	Inventory, Composition, Service

Domain Inventory

By Thomas Erl

How can services be delivered to maximize recomposition when enterprise-wide standardization is not possible?

Problem	Establishing a single enterprise service inventory may be unmanageable for some enterprises, and attempts to do so may jeopardize the success of an SOA adoption as a whole.
Solution	Services can be grouped into manageable, domain-specific service inventories, each of which can be independently standardized, governed, and owned.
Application	Inventory domain boundaries need to be carefully established.
Impacts	Standardization disparity between domain service inventories imposes transformation requirements and reduces the overall benefit potential of the SOA adoption.
Principles	Standardized Service Contract, Service Abstraction, Service Composability
Architecture	Enterprise, Inventory

Enterprise Inventory
By Thomas Erl

How can services be delivered to maximize recomposition?

Problem	Delivering services independently via different project teams across an enterprise establishes a constant risk of producing inconsistent service and architecture implementations, compromising recomposition opportunities.
Solution	Services for multiple solutions can be designed for delivery within a standardized, enterprise-wide inventory architecture wherein they can be freely and repeatedly recomposed.
Application	The enterprise service inventory is ideally modeled in advance, and enterprise-wide standards are applied to services delivered by different project teams.
Impacts	Significant up-front analysis is required to define an enterprise inventory blueprint and numerous organizational impacts result from the subsequent governance requirements.
Principles	Standardized Service Contract, Service Abstraction, Service Composability
Architecture	Enterprise, Inventory

Functional Decomposition
By Thomas Erl

*How can a large business problem be solved without having
to build a standalone body of solution logic?*

Problem	To solve a large, complex business problem a corresponding amount of solution logic needs to be created, resulting in a self-contained application with traditional governance and reusability constraints.
Solution	The large business problem can be broken down into a set of smaller, related problems, allowing the required solution logic to also be decomposed into a corresponding set of smaller, related solution logic units.
Application	Depending on the nature of the large problem, a service-oriented analysis process can be created to cleanly deconstruct it into smaller problems.
Impacts	The ownership of multiple smaller programs can result in increased design complexity and governance challenges.
Principles	n/a
Architecture	Service

Non-Agnostic Context

By Thomas Erl

How can single-purpose service logic be positioned as an effective enterprise resource?

Problem	Non-agnostic logic that is not service-oriented can inhibit the effectiveness of service compositions that utilize agnostic services.
Solution	Non-agnostic solution logic suitable for service encapsulation can be located within services that reside as official members of a service inventory.
Application	A single-purpose functional service context is defined.
Impacts	Although they are not expected to provide reuse potential, non-agnostic services are still subject to the rigors of service-orientation.
Principles	Standardized Service Contract, Service Composability
Architecture	Service

Service Encapsulation

By Thomas Erl

How can solution logic be made available as a resource of the enterprise?

Problem	Solution logic designed for a single application environment is typically limited in its potential to interoperate with or be leveraged by other parts of an enterprise.
Solution	Solution logic can be encapsulated by a service so that it is positioned as an enterprise resource capable of functioning beyond the boundary for which it is initially delivered.
Application	Solution logic suitable for service encapsulation needs to be identified.
Impacts	Service-encapsulated solution logic is subject to additional design and governance considerations.
Principles	n/a
Architecture	Service

Additional Reading for Planning & Governing Service-Orientation

The Four Pillars of Service-Orientation

The Seven Levels of Organizational Maturity

SOA Governance Controls

This appendix provides supplementary reading resources for the topics covered in the *Planning for and Governing SOA* section from Chapter 2. All content in this appendix is comprised of condensed versions of excerpts from the *SOA Governance: Governing Shared Servies On-Premise and in the Cloud* series title.

The Four Pillars of Service-Orientation

Service-orientation provides us with a well-defined method for shaping software programs into units of service-oriented logic that we can legitimately refer to as services. Each such service that we deliver takes us a step closer to achieving the desired target state represented by these strategic goals and benefits.

Proven practices, patterns, principles, and technologies exist in support of service-orientation. However, because of the distinctly strategic nature of the target state that service-orientation aims to establish, there are several fundamental critical success factors that act as common prerequisites for its successful adoption. These critical success factors are referred to as *pillars* because they collectively establish a sound and healthy foundation upon which to build, deploy, and govern services.

The four pillars of service-orientation are:

- *Teamwork* – Cross-project teams and cooperation are required.
- *Education* – Team members must communicate and cooperate based on common knowledge and understanding.
- *Discipline* – Team members must apply their common knowledge consistently.
- *Balanced Scope* – The extent to which the required levels of Teamwork, Education, and Discipline need to be realized is represented by a meaningful yet manageable scope.

The existence of these four pillars is considered essential to any SOA initiative. The absence of any one of these pillars to a significant extent introduces a major risk factor. If such an absence is identified in the early planning stages, it can warrant delaying with project until it has been addressed or the project's scope has been reduced.

Teamwork

Whereas traditional silo-based applications require cooperation among members of individual project teams, the delivery of services and service-oriented solutions requires cooperation across multiple project teams. The scope of the required teamwork is noticeably larger and can introduce new dynamics, new project roles, and the need to forge and maintain new relationships among  individuals and departments. Those on the overall SOA team need to trust and rely on each other; otherwise, the team will fail.

Education

A key factor to realizing the reliability and trust required by SOA team members is to ensure that they use a shared communications framework based on common vocabulary, definitions, concepts, methods, and a common understanding of the target state the team is collectively working to attain. To achieve this common understanding requires common education, not just in general topics pertaining to service-orientation, SOA, and service technologies, but also in specific principles, patterns, and practices, as well as established standards, policies, and methodology specific to the organization.

Combining the pillars of teamwork and education establishes a foundation of knowledge and an understanding of how to use that knowledge among members of the SOA team. The resulting clarity eliminates many of the common risks that have traditionally plagued SOA projects.

Discipline

A critical success factor for any SOA initiative is consistency in how knowledge and practices amongst a cooperative team are used and applied. To be successful as a whole, team members must therefore be disciplined in how they apply their knowledge and in how they  carry out their respective roles. Required measures of discipline are commonly expressed in methodology, modeling, and design standards, as well as governance precepts. Even with the best intentions, an educated and cooperative team will fail in the absence of discipline.

Balanced Scope

So far we've established that we need:

- cooperative teams that have...

- a common understanding and education pertaining to industry and enterprise-specific knowledge areas and that...

- we need to consistently cooperate as a team, apply our understanding, and follow a common methodology and standards in a disciplined manner.

In some IT enterprises, especially those with a long history of building silo-based applications, achieving these qualities can be challenging. Cultural, political, and various other forms of organizational issues can arise to make it difficult to attain the necessary organizational changes required by these three pillars. How then can they be realistically achieved? It all comes down to defining a balanced scope of adoption.

The scope of adoption needs to be meaningfully cross-silo, while also realistically manageable. This requires the definition of a balanced scope of adoption of service-orientation, a goal that can be directly mapped to the following SOA Manifesto guiding principle: *"The scope of SOA adoption can vary. Keep efforts manageable and within meaningful boundaries."*

Once a balanced scope of adoption has been defined, this scope determines the extent to which the other three pillars need to be established. Conversely, the extent to which you can realize the other three pillars will influence how you determine the scope (Figure B.1).

Common factors involved in determining a balanced scope include:

- cultural obstacles

- authority structures

- geography

- business domain alignment

- available stakeholder support and funding

- available IT resources

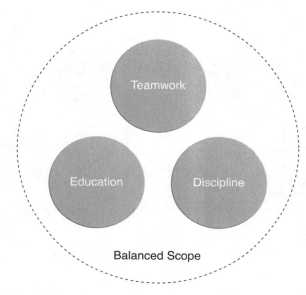

Figure B.1

The Balanced Scope pillar encompasses and sets the scope at which
the other three pillars are applied for a given adoption effort.

A single organization can choose one or more balanced adoption scopes (Figure B.2).
Having multiple scopes results in a domain-based approach to adoption. Each domain
establishes a boundary for an inventory of services. Among domains, adoption of service-orientation and the delivery of services can occur independently. This does not
result in application silos; it establishes meaningful service domains (also known as
"continents of services") within the IT enterprise.

The domain-based approach to the adoption of SOA and service-orientation originated
with the Domain Inventory pattern.

IT Enterprise

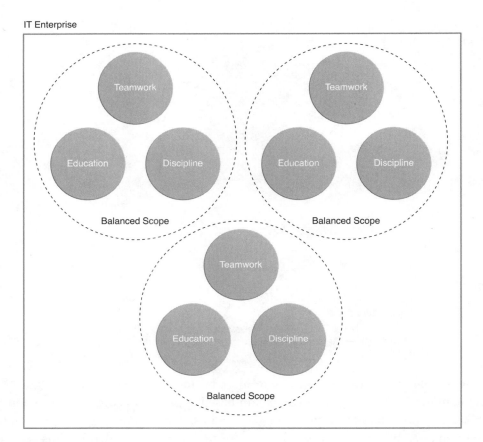

Figure B.2

Multiple balanced scopes can exist within the same IT enterprise. Each represents a separate service inventory that is independently standardized, owned, and governed.

The Seven Levels of Organizational Maturity

The following is a set of descriptions for the seven levels or organizational maturity that were introduced in Chapter 2. It is worth noting that the sequence in which some of these levels are intentionally or inadvertantly attained can vary, as shown in Figure B.3.

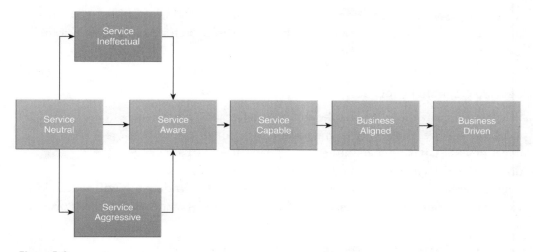

Figure B.3
Multiple balanced scopes can exist within the same IT enterprise. Each represents a separate service inventory that is independently standardized, owned, and governed.

Service Neutral Level

This level indicates that there may be an awareness of SOA and service-orientation within the organization, but no meaningful extent of teamwork, education, or discipline has been established or yet identified. Every organization begins at the Service Neutral level, as it represents the starting point in the evolutionary lifecycle. Whereas the Service Neutral level represents an absence of maturity because the organization has not yet proceeded with an adoption effort, the Service Ineffectual and Service Aggressive levels represent an absence of maturity during the adoption effort. Figure 4.3 illustrates this by positioning this level at the beginning of the lifecycle. From this point, an organization can either move on to the Service Ineffectual or Service Aggressive levels, or it can proceed to the Service Aware level.

Service Aware Level

When reaching the Service Aware level, it has been confirmed that the four pillars have been established, that relevant business requirements and goals are defined, and that the overall necessary organizational foundation for the SOA initiative is in place. Within this context, the term "service aware" does not refer to an IT enterprise becoming aware of SOA and service-orientation; it refers to an early planning stage that validates that the necessary foundations (pillars) and business direction for a planned SOA initiative are in place.

Service Capable Level

When the organization achieves the ability to deliver and govern services and service compositions in response to business automation requirements, it has reached the Service Capable level. An organization at this level will have avoided or overcome common adoption pitfalls and will therefore be positioned for a successful SOA initiative. It will have a skilled, well-trained team that has consistently delivered services within the required processes and regulations.

The principal risk at this level is that of stalling—remaining at a service capable level, without making further progress to move on to the Business Aligned level. This risk exists due to a potential sense of satisfaction with the current state of having services capable of composition in support of current business automation requirements. However, when those business requirements begin to change, it becomes necessary to ensure and maintain a high level of alignment, which is why a transition to the next level must always remain a goal.

Business Aligned Level

This level indicates that the organization has achieved meaningful alignment of (service-oriented) technology resources and current business automation requirements. In other words, the organization has successfully aligned services and service compositions with the current state of the business.

Attaining this state further implies that most or all of the services planned for a given service inventory have been delivered and are in operation. Therefore, the Business Aligned level represents a level of organizational maturity that has resulted in a relatively mature service inventory.

Business Driven Level

This evolutionary level represents a state where service-encapsulated technology resources are not just aligned with the current state of the business, but have proven to remain in alignment with how business requirements continue to change. This form of evolutionary alignment is accomplished via the repeated or augmented composition of services. This level therefore represents the highest level of maturity for a service inventory as well as the highest level of success for the overall SOA adoption effort. The Business Driven level can last indefinitely as the organization continues to leverage the strategic benefits of its services.

Service Ineffectual Level

The Service Ineffectual level occurs when an organization descends into a technological backwater where the IT enterprise delivers services as silo-based or bottom-up automation solutions under the pretense that it is adopting SOA. Services delivered during this level are generally not actual units of service-oriented logic. They are most likely single-purpose software programs labeled as services because they use a service technology (such as Web services, REST services, cloud-based services, etc.).

This level represents an IT initiative that, under the guise of "SOA", is tactically focused without much regard for service-orientation or the steps necessary to attain the strategic target state associated with SOA and service-oriented computing.

Service Aggressive Level

When an organization is Service Aggressive, it is usually because IT's enthusiasm for SOA and service technology has led to a proliferation of services that the business doesn't want or need; in some cases, the business may not even be aware of their existence. The Service Aggressive level is different from the Service Ineffectual level in that there may be a sincere intention to adopt SOA and service-orientation in support of strategic goals. However, due to lack of teamwork, education, or discipline or even blatant incompetence, the SOA initiative fails to align its technology in support of the business. This misalignment therefore severely limits the usefulness and longevity of delivered services.

> **NOTE**
>
> So many IT projects have fallen victim to this pitfall that it has tarnished the perception of "SOA" in general, leading to the need for the SOA Manifesto covered in Chapter 4.

SOA Governance Controls

An organization establishes governance to mitigate risk and to help advance its strategy, goals, and priorities. When the organization invests in an SOA initiative, it expects to gain benefits worth more than the cost of the investment. This return on investment is measured in terms of business outcomes, and, presumably, those outcomes reflect the organization's strategy, goals, and priorities. Therefore, the primary business goal for SOA governance is to ensure that an SOA initiative achieves its targeted business outcome.

An SOA governance system is the meta-decision system that an organization puts in place to control and constrain decision-making responsibilities related to the adoption and application of service-orientation. There are many practices, considerations, models, and frameworks that can comprise a meta-decision system suitable for SOA governance.

Let's take a closer look at the primary building blocks that comprise an IT governance system, all of which are required as part of an SOA governance system:

- *Precepts* – define the rules that govern decision-making
- *Processes* – coordinate precept-related decision-making activities
- *People* – assume roles and make decisions based on precepts
- *Metrics* – measure compliance to precepts

These building blocks can be collectively or individually referred to as *governance controls*.

Precepts

A *precept* is an authoritative rule of action. Precepts are the essence of governance because they determine who has authority to make decisions, establish constraints for those decisions, and prescribe consequences for non-compliance.

Precepts codify decision-making rules using:

- *Objectives* – broadly define a precept and establish its overarching responsibility, authority, and goals

- *Policies* – define specific aspects of a precept and establish decision-making constraints and consequences

- *Standards* – specify the mandatory formats, technologies, processes, actions, and metrics that people are required to use and carry out in order to implement one or more policies

- *Guidelines* – are non-mandatory recommendations and best practices

Processes

A process is an organized representation of a series of activities. It is important to make a distinction between governance processes and other types of processes related to IT. Governance processes provide a means by which to control decisions, enforce policies, and take corrective action in support of the governance system. Other processes, such as those employed to carry out project delivery stages, can be heavily influenced by governance precepts, but are not specifically processes that are directly related to carrying out the governance system. Technically, any process is considered a management activity, but a governance system is dependent on governance processes to ensure compliance with its precepts.

> **NOTE**
>
> Within some IT communities, the term "policy" is commonly used instead of "precept" in relation to governance systems. However, as just explained, a policy can technically be just one aspect of a precept. Also, even though a precept can contain standards, certain precepts themselves are considered standards. Therefore, it is important to not be confused when the precept name includes the word "standard" (such as Service Design Standard precept), and the precept itself further contains one or more standards that support corresponding precept policies.

An organization is likely to use a variety of processes to support its precepts. Some may be automated, while others require human effort. Automated processes can help coordinate tasks (such as steps required to collect data for approvals), but can still rely on people to make important decisions (such as making the actual approvals based on the presented data). Examples of decisions that typically cannot be automated include reviewing and assessing investment proposals, reviewing system and service designs, and selecting products and technologies.

People (Roles)

People (and groups of people) make decisions in accordance to and within the constraints stipulated by governance precepts. For a governance system to be successful, people must understand the intents and purposes of the precepts and they must understand and accept the responsibilities and authorities established by the precepts. Governance systems are therefore often closely associated with an organization's incentive system. This allows the organization to foster a culture that supports and rewards good behavior, while also deterring and punishing poor behavior.

When exploring the involvement of people in relation to governance systems, it is further necessary to identify the role or roles they assume. Organizational roles position people (and groups) in relation to governance models and further affect the relevance of precept compliance and enforcement. There are two ways that people can relate to precepts and processes: they can help author the precepts and processes and they can be dictated by their application.

Metrics

Metrics provide information that can be used to measure and verify compliance with precepts. The use of metrics increases visibility into the progress and effectiveness of the governance system. By analyzing metrics, we gain insight into the efficacy of governance rules and we can further discover whether particular policies or processes are too onerous or unreasonable. Metrics also measure trends, such as the number of violations and requests for waivers. A large number of waiver requests may indicate that a policy is not appropriate or effective.

Appendix C

Additional Reading for Cloud Computing

Goals and Benefits

Risks and Challenges

This appendix provides supplementary reading resources for the topics covered in the *Cloud Computing* section from Chapter 5. The content in this appendix is comprised of condensed versions of excerpts from the *Cloud Computing: Concepts, Technology & Architecture* series title.

Goals and Benefits

An organization that keeps automation solutions and associated IT resources on-premise as part of an in-house IT enterprise bears the responsibilities that come with this level of ownership and control.

The organization may be responsible for:

- establishing an enterprise infrastructure that can support the usage demands of the automation solutions and IT resources

- administering and upgrading IT resources to keep them current and supportive of automation solution requirements

- evolving and augmenting the IT enterprise in response to ongoing business change

Cloud computing provides alternatives for the developing, hosting, administration, and evolution of IT resources. The common benefits associated with adopting cloud computing are explained in this section.

Reduced Investments and Proportional Costs

Similar to a product wholesaler that purchases goods in bulk for lower price points, public cloud providers base their business model on the mass acquisition of IT resources that are then made available to cloud consumers via attractively priced leasing packages. This opens the door for organizations to gain access to powerful infrastructure without having to purchase it themselves.

The most common economic rationale for investing in cloud-based IT resources is in the reduction or outright elimination of up-front IT investments, namely hardware and software purchases and ownership costs. A cloud's Measured Usage characteristic represents a feature-set that allows measured operational expenditures (directly related to business performance) to replace anticipated capital expenditures. This is also referred to as proportional costs.

This minimization or elimination of up-front financial commitments allows enterprises to start small and accordingly increase the resource allocation as required. Moreover, the reduction of up-front capital expenses allows for the capital to be redirected to the core business investment. In its most basic form, opportunities to decrease costs are derived from the deployment and operation of large-scale data centers by major cloud providers. Such data centers are commonly located in destinations, where real estate, IT professionals, and network bandwidth can be obtained at lower costs, resulting in both capital and operational savings.

The same rationale applies to operating systems, middleware or platform software, and application software. Pooled IT resources are made available to and shared by multiple cloud consumers, resulting in increased or even the maximum possible utilization. Operational costs and inefficiencies can be further reduced by applying proven practices and patterns for optimizing cloud architectures, their management, and governance.

Common measurable benefits to cloud consumers include:

- On-demand access to pay-as-you-go computing resources on a short-term basis (such as processors by the hour), and the ability to release these computing resources when they are no longer needed.

- The perception of having unlimited computing resources that are available on demand, thereby reducing the need to prepare for provisioning.

- The ability to add or remove IT resources at a fine-grained level, such as modifying available storage disk space by single Gigabyte increments.

- Abstraction of the infrastructure so applications are not locked into devices or locations and can be easily moved if needed.

For example, a company with sizable batch-centric tasks can complete them as quickly as their application software can scale. Using 100 servers for one hour costs the same as using one server for 100 hours. This "elasticity" of IT resources, achieved without requiring steep initial investments to create a large-scale computing infrastructure, can be extremely compelling.

Despite the ease at which many identify the financial benefits of cloud computing, the actual economics can be complex to calculate and assess. The decision to proceed with a cloud computing adoption strategy will involve much more than a simple comparison between the cost of leasing a cloud-based server and the cost of purchasing a similar server. For example, the financial benefits of dynamic scaling and the risk transference of both over-provisioning (under-utilization) and under-provisioning (saturation) must also be accounted for.

> ### NOTE
>
> Another area of cost savings offered by clouds is the "as-a-service" usage model, whereby technical and operational implementation details of IT resource provisioning are abstracted from cloud consumers and packaged into "ready-to-use" or "off-the-shelf" solutions. These services-based products can simplify and expedite the development, deployment, and administration of IT resources when compared to performing equivalent tasks with on-premise solutions. The resulting savings in time and required IT expertise can be significant and can contribute to the justification of adopting cloud computing.

Increased Scalability

By providing pools of IT resources, along with tools and technologies designed to leverage them collectively, clouds can instantly and dynamically allocate IT resources to cloud consumers, on-demand or via the cloud consumer's direct configuration. This empowers cloud consumers to scale their cloud-based IT resources to accommodate processing fluctuations and peaks automatically or manually. Similarly, cloud-based IT resources can be released (automatically or manually) as processing demands decrease. A simple example of usage demand fluctuations throughout a 24-hour period is provided in Figure C.1.

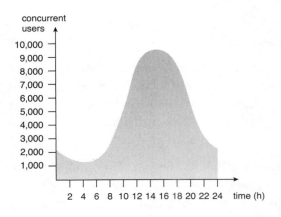

Figure C.1

An example of an organization's changing demand for an IT resource over the course of a day.

The inherent, built-in feature of clouds to provide flexible levels of scalability to IT resources is directly related to the aforementioned proportional costs benefit. Besides the evident financial benefit to the automated reduction of scaling, the ability of IT resources to always meet and fulfill unpredictable usage demands prevents the potential losses of business that can occur when usage thresholds have been met.

Increased Availability and Reliability

The availability and reliability of IT resources are directly associated with tangible business benefits. Outages limit the time an IT resource can be "open for business" for its customers, thereby limiting its usage and revenue-generating potential. Run-time failures that are not immediately correct can have a more significant impact in that they may occur during high-volume usage periods. Not only is the IT resource unable to respond to customer requests, its unexpected failure can decrease overall customer confidence.

A hallmark of the typical cloud environment is its intrinsic ability to provide extensive support for increasing the availability of a cloud-based IT resource to minimize or even eliminate outages, and for increasing its reliability so as to minimize the impact of run-time failure conditions.

Specifically:

- An IT resource with increased availability is accessible for longer periods of time (for example, 22 hours out of a 24-hour day). Cloud providers generally offer resilient IT resources for which they are able to guarantee high levels of availability.

- An IT resource with increased reliability is able to better avoid and recover from exception conditions. The modular architecture of cloud environments provides extensive failover support that increases reliability.

It is important that organizations carefully examine the SLAs offered by cloud providers when considering the leasing of cloud-based services and IT resources. Although many cloud environments offer remarkably high levels of availability and reliability, it comes down to the guarantees made in the SLA that typically represent the actual contractual obligations.

Risks and Challenges

Several of the most critical cloud computing challenges pertaining mostly to cloud consumers that use IT resources located in public clouds are presented and examined.

Increased Security Vulnerabilities

The moving of business data to the cloud means that the responsibility over data security becomes shared with the cloud provider. The remote usage of IT resources requires an expansion of trust boundaries by the cloud consumer to include the external cloud. It can be difficult to establish a security architecture that spans such a trust boundary without introducing vulnerabilities, unless cloud consumers and cloud providers happen to support the same or compatible security frameworks—which is highly unlikely.

Another consequence of overlapping trust boundaries relates to the cloud provider's privileged access to cloud consumer data. The extent to which the data is secure is now limited to the security controls and policies applied by both the cloud consumer and cloud provider. Furthermore, there can be overlapping trust boundaries from different cloud consumers due to the fact that cloud-based IT resources are commonly shared.

The overlapping of trust boundaries and the increased exposure of data can provide malicious cloud consumers (human and automated) with greater opportunities to attack IT resources and steal or damage business data.

Figure C.2 illustrates a scenario whereby two organizations accessing the same cloud service are required to extend their respective trust boundaries to the cloud, resulting in overlapping trust boundaries. It can be challenging for a cloud provider to offer security mechanisms that accommodate the security requirements of both cloud service consumers.

Reduced Operational Governance Control

Cloud consumers are usually allotted a level of governance control that is lower than that over on-premise IT resources. This reduced level of governance control can introduce risks associated with how the cloud provider operates its cloud, as well as the external connections that are required for communication between the cloud and the cloud consumer.

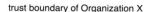

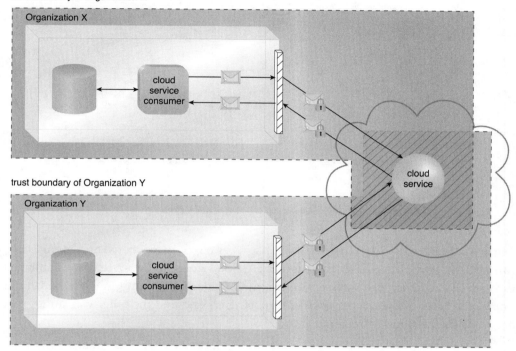

Figure C.2

Overlapping trust boundaries are an example of a cloud security threat.

Consider the following examples:

- An unreliable cloud provider may not maintain the guarantees it makes in the SLAs that were published for its cloud services.

- Greater geographic distances between the cloud consumer and cloud provider can require additional network hops that introduce fluctuating latency and potential bandwidth constraints.

The former scenario can further jeopardize the quality of cloud consumer solutions that are reliant on cloud services, as illustrated in Figure C.3.

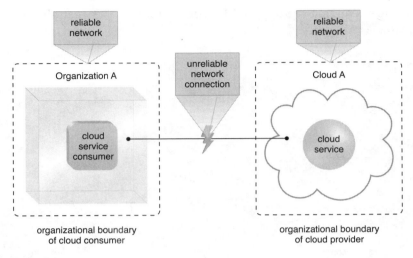

Figure C.3
An unreliable network connection is shown compromising the service level.

Legal contracts, when combined with SLAs, technology inspections, and monitoring, can mitigate governance risks and issues. A cloud governance system is established through SLAs, given the "as-a-service" nature of cloud computing. A cloud consumer must keep track of the actual service level being offered and the other warranties that are made by the cloud provider.

Limited Portability Between Cloud Providers

Due to a lack of established industry standards within the cloud computing industry, individual clouds are commonly proprietary to various extents. For cloud consumers that have custom-built solutions with dependencies on these proprietary environments, it can be challenging to move from one cloud provider to another.

Portability is a measure used to determine the impact of moving cloud consumer IT resources and data between clouds (Figure C.4).

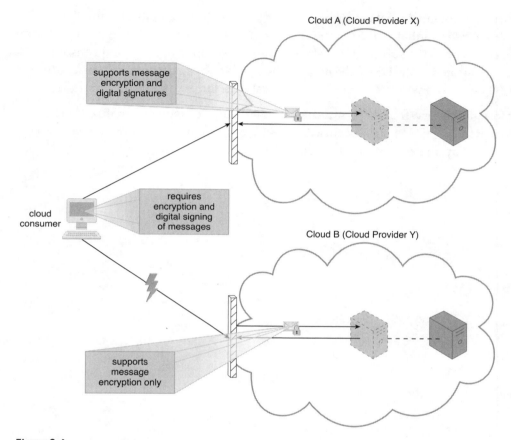

Figure C.4

A cloud consumer's application has a decreased level of portability when assessing a potential migration from Cloud A to Cloud B, because the cloud provider of Cloud B does not support the same security technologies as Cloud A.

Multi-Regional Compliance and Legal Issues

Third-party cloud providers will frequently establish data centers in affordable or convenient geographical locations. Cloud consumers will often not be aware of the physical location of their IT resources and data when hosted by public clouds. For some organizations, this can pose serious legal concerns pertaining to industry or government regulations that specify data privacy and storage policies. For example, some UK laws require personal data belonging to UK citizens to be kept within the physical borders of the United Kingdom.

Another potential legal issue pertains to the accessibility and disclosure of data. Countries have laws that require some types of data to be disclosed to certain government agencies or to the subject of the data. For example, a European cloud consumer's data that is located in the US can be more easily accessed by government agencies (due to the US Patriot Act) when compared to data located in European Union countries.

Most regulatory frameworks recognize that cloud consumer organizations are ultimately responsible for the security, integrity, and storage of their own data, even when it is held by an external cloud provider.

About the Authors

Thomas Erl

Thomas Erl is a top-selling IT author, founder of Arcitura Education, and series editor of the *Prentice Hall Service Technology Series from Thomas Erl*. With more than 175,000 copies in print worldwide, his books have become international bestsellers and have been formally endorsed by senior members of major IT organizations, such as IBM, Microsoft, Oracle, Intel, Accenture, IEEE, HL7, MITRE, SAP, CISCO, HP, and many others. As CEO of Arcitura Education Inc., Thomas has led the development of curricula for the internationally recognized Big Data Science Certified Professional (BDSCP), Cloud Certified Professional (CCP) and SOA Certified Professional (SOACP) accreditation programs, which have established a series of formal, vendor-neutral industry certifications obtained by thousands of IT professionals around the world. Thomas has toured more than 20 countries as a speaker and instructor. More than 100 articles and interviews by Thomas have been published in numerous publications, including The Wall Street Journal and CIO Magazine.

Clive Gee, PhD

Clive Gee has over 30 years' experience in the IT industry and has worked for IBM in both the UK and the United States, spending the majority of his career as a solution architect dedicated to the early customer implementations of emerging technologies such as object-orientation, mobile computing, and SOA. Clive has taken on the role of consulting architect on many customer engagements in the aerospace, manufacturing, and public sectors, as well as projects in the retail, transportation, telecommunications, insurance, and financial industries. He has a strong business focus and a track record of developing innovative and yet practical solutions to fulfill real business needs.

Over the last few years, Clive has turned his attention to SOA governance, a field in which he is considered to be a leading worldwide practitioner. He has led efforts with several major organizations in the United States, Japan, and Australia that were successful at establishing SOA Centers of Excellence and implementing effective governance in areas of service-orientation.

Clive is currently residing in Scotland's Northern Isles as a semi-retiree who still agrees to take part in the occasional project. He is a co-author of the book titled *SOA Governance: Achieving and Sustaining Business Agility* (IBM Press 2008), as well as another book from the *Prentice Hall Service Technology Series from Thomas Erl* titled *SOA Governance: Governing Shared Services On-Premise and in the Cloud*.

Jürgen Kress

An expert in middleware, Jürgen currently works at Oracle EMEA Alliances and Channels and is responsible for Oracle's EMEA fusion middleware partner business. He is the founder of the Oracle SOA & BPM, WebLogic Partner Communities, and the global Oracle Partner Advisory Councils. The Fusion Middleware Partner Community is home to over 5,000 members internationally as Oracle's most active and successful community, which Jürgen manages with monthly newsletters, Webcasts, and conferences. He also hosts the annual Fusion Middleware Partner Community Forums and Fusion Middleware Summer Camps, where more than 200 partners receive product updates, roadmap insights, and hands-on training supplemented by a variety of Web 2.0 tools like Twitter, discussion forums, online communities, blogs, and wikis. Jürgen is also a member of the steering board of the International SOA, Cloud + Service Technology Symposium, and is a frequent speaker at conferences that include the SOA & BPM Integration Days, JAX, UKOUG, OUGN, and OOP.

Berthold Maier

Berthold enjoys working for a wide portfolio of clients as a chief architect and enterprise architect, and possesses over 18 years of experience as a developer, coach, and architect in the building of complex mission-critical applications and in integration scenarios. Throughout his 11-year career at Oracle, Berthold has been given leading positions within the consulting division that notably included chief architect, a management position in which he assumed responsibility for reference architectures involving SOA and enterprise integration. Berthold is also the originator and architect of several frameworks around EAM and SOA, and is well-known as a conference speaker, book author, and magazine writer.

Hajo Normann

Hajo works for Accenture in the role of SOA & BPM Community of Practice lead in ASG and is responsible for the architecture and solution design of SOA/BPM projects, primarily acting as the interface between business and IT. He enjoys tackling organizational and technical challenges and motivating solutions in customer workshops, conferences, and publications. Together with Torsten Winterberg, Hajo leads the DOAG SIG Middleware and is an Oracle ACE director and active member of a global network within Accenture who is in regular contact with SOA/BPM architects from around the world.

Pethuru Raj

Pethuru possesses over 12 years of professional experience in the IT industry. In his academic career, he was granted international fellowships, JSPS and JST, to work as a postdoctoral researcher at two leading Japanese universities for three years. After earning a UGC-sponsored PhD degree from Anna University in Chennai, India, Pethuru obtained a CSIR fellowship to work as a research associate in the department of Computer Science and Automation at the Indian Institute of Science in Bangalore. Pethuru has worked as an application architect for eight years and a product architect for four years, leveraging the opportunities that came his way to become specialized in the business domains of telecommunications, retail, government, energy, and healthcare.

Prior to his career at Wipro Consulting, Pethuru spent one year as the enterprise architect at Sify Software Ltd. and over a year and a half as a lead architect in Bosch's corporate research division. During his three years as a senior architect for the Oracle Fusion Middleware Practice of Wipro Technologies, Pethuru become well-versed in emerging technologies like cloud computing, SOA, event-driven architecture, and enterprise architecture. He has also developed a keen understanding of Big Data computing (Hadoop), realtime cloud analytics, and machine-to-machine (M2M) integration, as well as high-performance system design and various smartphone applications. Pethuru has authored chapters for a number of technology-centric books in collaboration with internationally acclaimed professors, and is author of a book titled *Cloud Enterprise Architecture* that is published by CRC Press.

Leo Shuster

Leo has directed efforts in enterprise architecture and SOA strategy and execution for a number of organizations, including the National City Corporation, Ohio Savings Bank, and Progressive Insurance. He currently holds the position of director, IT Architecture at Nationwide Insurance, and possesses almost 20 years of IT experience. Throughout his career, Leo has performed in a variety of roles that span all aspects of the software development lifecycle and IT management. As a result, Leo has gained expertise in enterprise and application architecture, SOA, and IT governance and transformation, as well as platform modernization, process management and reengineering, and strategic planning, among many other areas. He frequently shares this knowledge with the IT community through articles and blog posts. Leo holds an MS in computer science and engineering from the Case Western Reserve University, and an MBA from the Cleveland State University.

Leo has presented on enterprise architecture, SOA, BPM, and related topics for groups of all sizes at various industry events and conferences. He is a co-author of the book titled *SOA Governance: Governing Shared Services On-Premise and in the Cloud*, which is a part of the *Prentice Hall Service Technology Series from Thomas Erl*. Leo regularly discusses advanced software architecture topics on his blog, which can be viewed at http://leoshuster.blogspot.com.

Bernd Trops

Since the launch of his career in the mid-90s, Bernd has worked as a system engineer, SOA architect, and coach on countless OO and SOA projects for a range of companies that include GemStone, Brokat, WebGain, and Oracle. During his time at Oracle, Bernd held the position of SOA architect and was primarily involved in large-scale initiatives. One notable project under his belt is the Deutsche Post Service-Backbone, which comprises the foundation of the Talend ESB. In his current role of principal solution architect at Talend, Bernd is closely involved in technical architecture and the design of complex IT solutions.

Bernd has presented at a number of industry conferences during his career, such as the SOA Symposium, Oracle Open World, JAX, and OOP. Bernd is co-author of *SOA Design Patterns* and *SOA Speizial*, as well as cofounder of the Mason of SOA.

Clemens Utschig-Utschig

Clemens is currently heading Marketing & Sales Architecture at Boehringer Ingelheim, one of the world's leading pharmaceutical companies, at its corporate headquarters in Germany, focusing on implementing the digital revolution and consolidating the global landscape onto standard platforms. Before joining Marketing and Sales he ran the global master data management program inside BI's Shared Service Center – developing the global process templates for customer, vendor and material maintainance, deploying those into BI's network and providing global transactional services from Brazil to China. Prior to joining Boehringer Ingelheim, Clemens fostered a ten-year career at Oracle as a platform architect on the SOA/BPM development team, helping clients establish enterprise-wide SOA. He also drove the development of several platform components, such as the Weblogic SCA container and the Spring Service Engine.

Philip Wik

Philip is currently a DBA for Redflex Traffic Systems. With more than 30 years of experience, Philip has worked as an architect, analyst, integrator, and developer for prominent leading companies such as JPMorgan Chase, Wells Fargo, and American Express, as well as Honeywell, Boeing, and Intel.

Having received training and education on three different continents, Philip has a robust multinational orientation and has led a number of offshore teams. He has also published two business books titled *How to Do Business With the People's Republic of China* and *How to Buy and Manage Income Property*, and is a frequent article contributor to the online *Service Technology Magazine*.

Torsten Winterberg

Active in several roles at OPITZ CONSULTING with strong dedication to delivering value to customers, Torsten is part of the business development and innovation department. In this role, he focuses on identifying and evaluating emerging trends and technologies with the aim of delivering innovative and differentiated solutions to customers. Also a director of the competence center for integration and business process solutions, Torsten is following his passion for building the best delivery unit for customer solutions in the areas of SOA and BPM.

Torsten has extensive experience as a developer, coach, and architect in building complex mission-critical Java EE applications, although his proficiency and passion actually lie in the design and architecture of complex IT systems involving BPMN, BPEL, ESB, BAM, and SOA in general. A recognized speaker in the German Java and Oracle communities, Torsten has written numerous articles on SOA/BPM-related topics and is part of the Oracle ACE director team, leading the DOAG middleware community.

Index

X-Y-Z

ABOUT THE SERIES

The Prentice Hall Service Technology Series from Thomas Erl aims to provide the IT industry with a consistent level of unbiased, practical, and comprehensive guidance and instruction in the areas of service technology application and innovation. Each title in this book series is authored in relation to other titles so as to establish a library of complementary knowledge. Although the series covers a broad spectrum of service technology-related topics, each title is authored in compliance with common language, vocabulary, and illustration conventions so as to enable readers to continually explore cross-topic research and education.

servicetechbooks.com/community

ABOUT THE SERIES EDITOR

Thomas Erl is a best-selling IT author, the series editor of the Prentice Hall Service Technology Series from Thomas Erl, and the editor of the Service Technology Magazine. As CEO of Arcitura™ Education Inc. and in cooperation with CloudSchool.com™ and SOASchool.com®, Thomas has led the development of curricula for the internationally recognized SOA Certified Professional (SOACP) and Cloud Certified Professional (CCP) accreditation programs, which have established a series of formal, vendor-neutral industry certifications. Thomas has toured over 20 countries as a speaker and instructor. Over 100 articles and interviews by Thomas have been published in numerous publications, including the Wall Street Journal and CIO Magazine.

**SOA Governance:
Governing Shared
Services On-Premise
& in the Cloud**
by Stephen Bennett,
Thomas Erl,
Clive Gee,
Robert Laird,
Anne Thomas Manes,
Robert Schneider,
Leo Shuster,
Andre Tost,
Chris Venable

ISBN: 0138156751
Hardcover, 675 pages

**SOA with REST:
Principles, Patterns
& Constraints for
Building Enterprise
Solutions with REST**
by Raj Balasu
-bramanian,
Benjamin Carlyle,
Thomas Erl,
Cesare Pautasso

ISBN: 0137012519
Hardcover, 577 pages

**Cloud Computing:
Concepts, Technology
& Architecture**
by Thomas Erl,
Zaigham Mahmood,
Ricardo Puttini

ISBN: 9780133387520
Hardcover, 528 pages

**SOA with Java:
Realizing Service
-Orientation with
Java Technologies**
by Thomas Erl,
Satadru Roy,
Philip Thomas,
Andre Tost

ISBN: 9780133859034
Hardcover, 592 pages

**Next Generation
SOA: A Concise
Introduction to
Service Technology &
Service-Orientation**
by Thomas Erl, Clive
Gee, Jürgen Kress,
Berthold Maier, Hajo
Normann, Pethuru Raj,
Leo Shuster, Bernd
Trops, Clemens
Utschig-Utschig, Philip
Wik, Torsten Winterberg

ISBN: 9780133859041
Paperback, 208 pages

**Cloud Computing
Design Patterns**
by Thomas Erl,
Amin Naserpour

Coming Soon

**Service-Oriented
Architecture: A
Field Guide to
Integrating XML
and Web Services**
by Thomas Erl

ISBN: 0131428985
Paperback, 534 pages

**Service-Oriented
Architecture:
Concepts, Technology
& Design**
by Thomas Erl

ISBN: 0131858580
Hardcover, 760 pages

**SOA Principles of
Service Design**
by Thomas Erl

ISBN: 0132344823
Hardcover, Full-Color,
573 pages

**Web Service
Contract Design &
Versioning for SOA**
by Thomas Erl,
Anish Karmarkar,
Priscilla Walmsley,
Hugo Haas,
Umit Yalcinalp,
Canyang Kevin Liu,
David Orchard,
Andre Tost,
James Pasley

ISBN: 013613517X
Hardcover, 826 pages

SOA Design Patterns
by Thomas Erl

ISBN: 0136135161
Hardcover, Full-Color,
865 pages

**SOA with .NET
& Windows
Azure: Realizing
Service-Orientation
with the Microsoft
Platform**
by David Chou,
John deVadoss,
Thomas Erl, Nitin Gandhi,
Hanu Kommalapati,
Brian Loesgen,
Christoph Schittko,
Herbjorn Wilhelmsen,
Mickey Williams

ISBN: 0131582313
Hardcover, 893 pages

SOA & Cloud Computing Training & Certification

SOA Certified Professional (SOACP)

Content from this book and other series titles has been incorporated into the SOA Certified Professional (SOACP) program, an industry-recognized, vendor-neutral SOA certification curriculum developed by author Thomas Erl in cooperation with industry experts and academic communities and provided by SOASchool.com and training partners.

The SOA Certified Professional curriculum is comprised of a collection of 23 courses and labs that can be taken with or without formal testing and certification. Training can be delivered anywhere in the world by Certified Trainers. A comprehensive self-study program is available for remote, self-paced study, and exams can be taken world-wide via Prometric testing centers.

Dozens of public workshops are scheduled every quarter around the world by regional training partners.

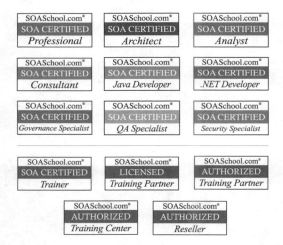

All courses are reviewed and revised on a regular basis to stay in alignment with industry developments.

For more information, visit: **www.soaschool.com**

www.soaworkshops.com • www.soaselfstudy.com

Cloud Certified Professional (CCP)

The Cloud Certified Professional (CCP) program, provided by CloudSchool.com, establishes a series of vendor-neutral industry certifications dedicated to areas of specialization in the field of cloud computing. Also founded by author Thomas Erl, this program exists independently from the SOASchool.com courses, while preserving consistency in terminology, conventions, and notation. This allows IT professionals to study cloud computing topics separately or in combination with SOA topics, as required.

The Cloud Certified Professional curriculum is comprised of 21 courses and labs, each of which has a corresponding Prometric exam. Private and public training workshops can be provided throughout the world by Certified Trainers. Self-study kits are further available for remote, self-paced study and in support of instructor-led workshops.

All courses are reviewed and revised on a regular basis to stay in alignment with industry developments.

For more information, visit: **www.cloudschool.com**

www.cloudworkshops.com • www.cloudselfstudy.com

PROMETRIC

SOASchool.com and CloudSchool.com exams offered world-wide through Prometric testing centers (www.prometric.com/arcitura)

Arcitura™
the IT education company